GLOBETROTTER
TRAVEL GUIDE

MOZAMBIQUE

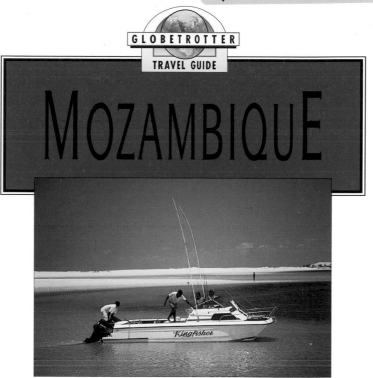

MIKE SLATER

NEW
HOLLAND

GLOBETROTTER
TRAVEL GUIDE

*** Highly recommended
** Recommended
* See if you can

First edition published in 1997
by New Holland (Publishers) Ltd
London • Cape Town • Sydney • Singapore

24 Nutford Place
London W1H 6DQ
United Kingdom

80 McKenzie Street
Cape Town 8001
South Africa

3/2 Aquatic Drive
Frenchs Forest, NSW 2086
Australia

ISBN 1 85368 425 2

Managing Editor: Mariëlle Renssen
Editors: Susannah Coucher, Claudia Dos Santos
Picture Researcher: Sonya Cupido
Design and DTP: Sonya Cupido
Cartographer: William Smuts
Compiler: Elaine Fick

Reproduction by cmyk pre-press, Cape Town
Printed and bound in Hong Kong by South China
Printing Company (1988) Limited

The author wishes to thank Etienne Marais,
who wrote the fact panel on p. 47, and Emina
of the Fishermen's Deli in Johannesburg for her
clarification regarding the sizing and preparation
of prawns. For the history section of this book,
extensive reference was made to Malyn Newitt's
A History of Mozambique (*see* p. 126).

Photographic Credits:
Anthony Bannister Photo Library/Andrew Bannister,
cover (bottom right), pages 11, 25, 64, 83, 91; **Gerald
Cubitt**, pages 9, 10; **Peter Kirchhoff**, pages 14, 34;
Photo Access (*Getaway*)/Jackie Nel, pages 19, 33
(top), 44; **Photo Access (*Getaway*)/David Steele**,
cover (bottom left), title page, pages 4, 8, 21, 27, 28,
47, 50, 55, 80, 81 (top and bottom); **Photo Access
(*Getaway*)/Patrick Wagner**, pages 7, 18, 38, 49, 76;
Mike Slater, cover (top left and top right), pages
17, 20, 22, 30, 33 (bottom), 35, 36, 40, 41, 48, 51–53,
58, 66–69, 71–73, 82, 85, 92, 94, 95, 96 (top), 99, 102,
109–117; **Ariadne van Zandbergen**, pages 6, 13,
15, 23, 24, 26, 29, 37, 39, 54, 61–63, 65, 70, 78, 79,
88, 93, 96 (bottom), 97, 100, 101, 103, 106, 118
(top and bottom), 119.

Cover Photographs:
Top left: *A reminder of the colonial past may be found
in Palace Square on Mozambique Island.*
Top right: *A timeless sight – a dhow gliding across the
tranquil waters of Nacala Bay.*
Bottom left: *An aerial view cannot do justice to splendid
Benguerra, one of the Bazaruto Archipelago's islands.*
Bottom right: *A child of the Makua tribe wears a
cosmetic face mask made from the fibre of the* nciro *tree.*
Title page: *A sport fishing boat returns to the beautiful
white shore of Benguerra Island.*

CONTENTS

1
Introducing Mozambique

From the overgrown remnants of **Portuguese outposts** along the mighty Zambezi to the ancient, mysterious **Mwenu Mutapa kingdom** and the enchanting and unique **Mozambique Island**, Mozambique offers an enticing and fascinating blend of cultures.

Arab dhows and modern **speedboats** crisscross the translucent tropical waters of a coral-fringed coastline, where **scuba-diving** opportunities rival the world's best. One of the lasting legacies of **Portuguese** and **Arab** traders and colonists are the colourful settlements found along the coast. Maputo, Inhambane, Beira, Quelimane and Pemba display a variety of architectural styles – from **Manueline** (*see* p. 27) to gaudy 1930s-inspired **Art Deco**.

So far, fortune-seekers have failed in their quest to find the legendary mines of **King Solomon**, said to contain hoards of gold, yet the stunning diversity of coastal, riverine, mountain, and forest environments are Mozambique's real treasure trove – home to a splendid array of fauna and flora – interspersed with traditional villages.

Although sadly neglected during the years of civil upheaval, the **Gorongosa National Park**, **Maputo Elephant Reserve** and **Bazaruto Archipelago** have been rehabilitated, while tropical island gems like **Magaruque**, **Benguerra** and **Bazaruto** offer seclusion, luxurious accommodation and excellent diving, fishing and bird-watching.

Whether your visit finds you on one of the endless deserted beaches or diving off the **coral isles**, you will discover a country filled with the enchanting sights and soothing sounds of Africa.

TOP ATTRACTIONS

*** **Bazaruto Archipelago:** luxury lodges and interesting dives away from the crowds.
*** **Maputaland:** elephants migrating along ancient trails; diving with dolphins.
** **Mozambique Island:** former capital of the country; has a 16th-century Portuguese fortress; wonderful ambience.
** **Wimbe beach**, **Pemba:** overlooking a picture-perfect inland bay.
* **Lake Cahora Bassa:** a vast population of crocodiles and hippo; great tigerfishing.

Opposite: *Splendid coral reefs are accessible from the hotel on Magaruque Island.*

Right: *The looming peak of Mt Namuli, Mozambique's second-highest mountain.*
Opposite: *Snorkelling in the crystal-clear water of the 'aquarium' off Benguerra Island's Two-Mile Reef.*

THE ZAMBEZI DELTA

• Width: 105km (65 miles) from Chinde in the north to Rio Mungari in the south.
• Area: the river divides at Marromeu; the delta covers 4000km² (1544 sq miles).
• Steam engines: the sugar plantations were served by narrow-gauge railway until 1978. The system now lies derelict, but the steam engines on the tracks near Chinde and Marromeu await inspection by enthusiasts.

VITAL STATISTICS

• Location: Between 26°52'S–21°27'S and 30°31'E–40°51'E.
• Area: 799,380km² (308,561 sq miles).
• Highest point: Mt Binga, 2436m (7993ft).
• Highest-lying province: Niassa; lowest is Sofala.
• Warmest town: Tete (28°C; 82°F); coolest town is Lichinga (18°C; 64°F).
• Largest river: Zambezi; length in Mozambique is 820km (510 miles).
• Largest bay: Pemba, at 3900km² (1505 sq miles).
• Deepest harbour: Nacala, at 300m (984ft).

THE LAND

Mozambique borders on South Africa and Swaziland to the south, Zimbabwe to the west and Zambia and Malawi in the northwest. The Rovuma River forms the remote boundary with Tanzania. The Indian Ocean's Mozambique Channel flanks a splendid coastline which is over 2500km (1554 miles) long. The south of the country is characterized by the extensive, well-treed savanna of the **Mozambican Plain**, where altitudes rarely range above 200m (656ft). The **Mozambican Plateau** dominates the central and northern regions, where rugged highlands are deeply incised by river valleys, and peaks such as **Binga** and **Gorongosa** in Manica, **Chiperone** in Zambezia, **Namuli** in Nampula and **Unango** in Niassa are located.

Most of Mozambique's tourist destinations are located along the southern coastline, or tucked away on islands such as **Inhaca** and the unique **Bazaruto Archipelago**, yet the interior, from the hot springs of Zambezia province and the granite domes of Nampula to the **Gorongosa forests** and **Quissico lakes**, is not without attractions.

Mountains and Rivers

Mozambique is cleft by the wide valley of the languid **Zambezi River**, which has gathered runoff from five countries and coursed over 3000km (1864 miles) before entering Mozambique at Feira. Here it is temporarily tamed by the 270km (168-mile) **Lake Cahora Bassa** with its 160m (525ft) wall and the potential to generate 4000 megawatts of hydroelectricity. Below the dam wall the river passes under the bridges of Tete and Sena before dispersing some 600km (373 miles) downstream into the myriad channels of its 100km-wide (62-mile) delta.

Other major rivers that flow through Mozambique are the crocodile-infested **Incomáti**, **Limpopo** and **Save** in the south and the **Licungo**, **Ligonha**, **Lúrio**, **Lugenda** and **Rovuma** in the north. The latter deserves more than a mention: not only does it form Mozambique's frontier with Tanzania, it also remains a formidable barrier. It isn't spanned by a single bridge and there is no vehicle ferry to afford overland access to or from the north – crossings of the Rovuma are possible by dugout canoe only.

The 2436m (7993ft) **Binga Peak** in the Chimanimani sandstone range ranks as Mozambique's highest mountain, while the granite crags of **Mount Unango** in Niassa present a challenge even to the most accomplished of rock-climbers. Religious ceremonies take place in caves on the slopes of **Mount Namuli** in Zambezia. In northern Tete province, which is notorious for its sticky tropical climate, the slopes of **Mount Dómuè** and the **Moravian Plateau** provide welcome relief from the oppressive heat.

Seas and Shores

Over 1200 species of fish have been identified in the coastal waters of Mozambique, most of which inhabit the extensive **coral reefs** that line the coast, particularly off **Maputaland**, around **Inhaca Island**, in the area of **Inhambane** and **Pebane** and along the **Querimba Archipelago** in the far north. Kingfish, mackerel, and tuna, a vital link in the food chain of the ocean and a popular catch with the locals, are attracted to the nourishment provided by the corals and their associated sealife. In terms of the

MOUNTAINS OF MYSTERY

● **Gorongosa:** a wonderland of diverse habitats; home to a marvellous variety of rare birds including buntings, canaries and orioles.
● **Chiperone:** named for the icy winds that blow off its summit, this peak rises out of a steamy, trackless jungle.
● **Namuli:** animists pay tribute to spirits in the hidden caves near the summit.
● **Unango:** in a remote part of Mozambique; a climber's challenge of sheer granite walls and precipitous exposed cliffs.
● **Binga:** Mozambique's highest point, straddling the border with Zimbabwe.

Opposite: *Storm clouds gather over the Gorongosa National Park.*
Below: *Atmospheric sunsets like this are common at Benguerra Island Lodge.*

variety of marine organisms, Mozambique's reefs are on a par with Australia's magnificent Great Barrier Reef, except that they are far less crowded and commercialized. Mozambique's superb reefs are delicate and as yet unspoilt marine wildernesses, their beauty and commercial value increasing the urgent need for formal protection.

South of the **Save River**, the coast is characterized by a string of inland lakes not fed by rivers and cut off from the sea by high parabolic (bowl-shaped) dunes stabilized by vegetation. The largest expanses of water in this coastal lake zone are lakes **Uembje** (Bilene), **Quissico** and **Inharrime**. Travellers on the main road between Maputo and Inhambane will be treated to scenic views from convenient vantage points.

Climate

Two major factors influencing Mozambique's climate are the warm Indian Ocean current moving south from the equator, and the altitude of the Mozambican Plateau. Temperatures along the coast and in the lower-lying areas of the plain and the Zambezi valley increase as one moves further north. Mozambique experiences **rain** mainly during **November–April**, while **August** is the **driest** month in most areas. The **wettest** provinces are **Niassa** (Metangula has 300mm, or 12in, during March)

and **Cabo Delgado** (Pemba has some 260mm, or 10in, between December–February). The **driest** part of the country is **Pafúri** where average annual precipitation rarely reaches 300mm (12in).

COMPARATIVE CLIMATE CHART	MAPUTO				BEIRA				LICHINGA			
	SUM	AUT	WIN	SPR	SUM	AUT	WIN	SPR	SUM	AUT	WIN	SPR
	JAN	APR	JULY	OCT	JAN	APR	JULY	OCT	JAN	APR	JULY	OCT
MAX TEMP. °C	31	25	21	25	34	29	22	27	25	20	19	23
MIN TEMP. °C	27	21	18	20	29	26	19	23	20	16	12	20
MAX TEMP. °F	88	77	70	77	93	84	72	81	77	68	66	73
MIN TEMP. °F	81	70	64	68	84	79	66	73	68	61	54	68
RAINFALL in	3	2	1.5	1.5	6	4	0.9	0.7	5	3	0.4	0
RAINFALL mm	75	55	40	40	144	110	25	20	120	80	10	0

Tropical Cyclones

The tropical cyclone is one of the most powerful and potentially destructive forms of atmospheric circulation. Falling just outside the region between 8°S–15°S, where the Indian Ocean temperatures are above 27°C (81°F), the **Mozambique Channel** experiences cyclones every few years, few of which move further south than Nacala.

Recent cyclones which have wreaked destruction on the northern Mozambique coastline were **Demoina** in 1984, **Nadia** in 1994, and **Gretelle** and **Josie** during 1997.

Plant Life

Much of Mozambique's temperate rainforests such as the ones around Dondo, Nova Vanduzi and Gogói have been devastated by logging and slash-and-burn agriculture. Yet magnificent **mopane woodlands** still dominate the southern plains, where battered old **baobab trees** flourish around Funhalouro in Inhambane province and along the northern coastline. Both species are important food sources: protein-rich mopane worms are widely eaten, while young baobabs are edible in their entirety.

The **woodland mahogany**, or *nkuhlu*, is widely distributed throughout Mozambique. Its spread is often greater than its height and can sometimes be seen to shelter an entire African *kraal* (homestead).

MANGROVE: TREE OF THE TIDES

Mangroves (*Rhizophoraceae*) are unique in their ability to flourish in tidal estuaries, due to rooting systems both above and below the ground. Breathing roots absorb vital nitrogen directly from the air, while the seeds germinate on the tree. Unfortunately, the mangrove's delicate, muddy habitat is now threatened as ground is drained to make way for new development. Mozambique's four species of mangrove still thrive at the **Save River** mouth, on the **Zambezi delta** and around **Quelimane**.

Right: *Impala antelope gather on a dry plain in the Gorongosa National Park.*
Opposite: Padrãos *(stone pillars) like this one were erected by Vasco da Gama.*

MERMAIDS

The dugong's Latin name, *Sirenia*, derives from the mythical Sirens of Greek folk-lore who lured lovesick sailors to rocky shoals. These tales may have originated due to the fact that **dugongs**, who look similar to walruses, suckle their live-born young from teats that are situated high on the mother's chest. Slow, sluggish and unafraid of humans, dugongs were hunted almost to extinction for their succulent flesh; however, recent studies indicate that they still occur and probably even breed around the **Bazaruto Archipelago**, and along the **Inhambane** and **Zambezia coasts**.

GORONGOSA UNDER FIRE

Gorongosa National Park was the base of the opposition **Renamo** movement from 1980–86. The soldiers had to survive by hunting and the wildife suffered severely. International attempts are currently underway to reintroduce herds of elephant, buffalo and other game, and visitors are already able to sip sundowners overlooking the waterhole at **Chitengo camp**.

Wildlife

Although the devastation of Mozambique's wildlife is unprecedented in Africa in recent times, programmes to reintroduce those species which attract tourists are now gathering momentum. **Elephant** can be viewed in the extreme south (Futi channel), and in the far north along the banks of the Rovuma River. **Rhino**, **buffalo**, **lion** and **leopard** exist, albeit in very small and threatened numbers, in the Gorongosa and Zambezi delta regions.

Sea mammals were less severely affected by the war and **whales**, **dolphins** and **dugongs** may be spotted in the vicinity of Ponta Malongane, Inhambane and Linga Linga.

Mozambique's birdlife is exceptionally varied. In excess of 900 species have been spotted south of the Zambezi. Favoured viewing spots are the Mount Gorongosa region, Gurué and Milange in Zambezia, Metangula and Cobúè in Niassa, and the Maputo Elephant Reserve.

Conserving Mozambique's Natural Heritage

The pitiful state of **Gorongosa National Park**, once rated among the best of Africa's wildlife sanctuaries, is indicative of the desperate position of Mozambique's fauna. Of six proclaimed parks in Mozambique (Banhine, Zinave, Gorongosa, Bazaruto Archipelago, Gili and Niassa) only Gorongosa and the Archipelago are ready to receive visitors. The **Elephant Reserve** across Maputo Bay was the first of the mainland parks to be rehabilitated, and may be visited by arrangement with **Nkomati Safaris** in Maputo.

HISTORY IN BRIEF

About 2000 years ago, climatic shifts caused the Sahara Desert of North Africa to expand southward, triggering a wave of **migration** from northwest Africa through the equatorial regions to southeast Africa. Northern Bantu-speaking tribes clashed with the nomadic hunter-gatherers of the south and displaced them. By the time **Arab traders** first landed on Mozambique 's offshore islands, around AD300, the aboriginal mainland inhabitants had been absorbed into Bantu society. Muslim traders, masters of the nuances of African trade and cultural practices, established alliances with tribes through intermarriage.

Vasco da Gama is generally honoured as the 'discoverer' of Mozambique. The span of coast which Da Gama's small fleet of four vessels passed on Christmas day 1497, was named **Natal**. Early in 1498 he anchored off an estuary near Inharrime in Inhambane province.

From AD300–1500, none of the Indian Ocean powers maintained a fleet and so they were helpless when Portuguese warships arrived at Sofala and Mozambique Island in the early 16th century. After erecting a fort here, Portuguese soldiers began demanding 'duties' on the cloth, ivory and gold leaving the area.

The Mwenu Mutapa

Portuguese traders were largely ignorant of the interior, but desperately desired to eclipse Spanish successes in the Americas, and so fabricated the myth of a fabulously rich empire, **Monomotapa**. During the 18th century it was not so much the promise of untold wealth that motivated the Portuguese Crown to pacify the tribes of the interior, but rather the murders of several missionaries and traders.

> ### SOSHANGANE, FATHER OF A NATION
>
> Southern Mozambique had for centuries been the home of the **Tsonga**; the origins of the **Shangaan** nation, however, lie in the more recent past. During the expansionist wars of Zulu king **Shaka**, Chief Soshangane and his people fled into Mozambique, where they clashed with and subsequently conquered the **Ronga** tribe. Though his warriors were not in the same league as Shaka's *impi*, Soshangane surprised himself by defeating a formidable Zulu army which had crossed the Pongola River in 1828. The battle spelt disaster for Shaka who was murdered by his half-brother that same year. Soshangane's spears, by contrast, glinted ever brighter in the Mozambican sun, where the Shangaan still prosper today.

HISTORICAL CALENDAR

2000BC Nomadic hunter-gatherers inhabit the region.
200BC–AD300 Bantu tribes displace indigenous people.
c300 Persian–Arab communities on Ibo/Mozambique islands.
1497–98 Da Gama lands at Mozambique en route to India.
1507–15 Portuguese erect a fort on Mozambique Island; tribute demanded from Arabs.
1510 Influence of Mwenu Mutapa kingdom gives rise to Monomotapa myth.
1560s Quelimane indicated on Portuguese maps.
1570–1600 Portuguese traders attacked along lower Zambezi River.

1709 Portuguese captaincies established at Sena, Tete, Zumbo and Manica.
1752 Government of Mozambique is separated from Goa. Portuguese secretariat established on Mozambique Island.
1781 Huge *prazos* (land leases) granted to Portuguese settlers who then resist Portuguese authority for nearly 150 years.
1808 Madagascan pirates raid Ibo and Mozambique islands.
1830 Slave trade between Mozambique/Brazil at a peak.
1891 Anglo–Portuguese treaty defines colonial borders.
1933 Mozambique becomes a 'de jure' province of Portugal.

1940–60 Immigration raises settler population to 100,000.
1960 Frelimo supporters massacred at Mueda; liberation struggle begins.
1974 Socialist junta replaces fascist regime in Portugal and cedes colonial territories.
1975 Flag of independent Mozambique raised in Maputo.
1977 Renamo formed by Rhodesian Secret Service.
1984 Nkomati Accord ends South African support of Renamo troops.
1992 Renamo and Frelimo sign peace treaty in Rome.
1994 Frelimo wins elections; Joaquim Chissano is President.

Portuguese Expansion and Local Resistance

By 1550, the Portuguese had wrested the coastal trading monopoly from the Arabs. The coastal forts needed to guard their dominion, however, were disease-ridden, the pay was low, discipline oppressive and Portuguese women a rarity. Men frequently ventured inland to trade firearms, and married the daughters of chiefs just like their Islamic predecessors. These opportunists had no official sanction and were largely ignored by the Portuguese authorities, until the murder, in 1561, of Gonçalo da Silveira, a fanatical Castilian missionary bent on the conversion of the Monomotapa. His murder came at a time when Portugal was looking to place more people under its land tax umbrella. In 1571 the Portuguese king sent a consort with presents (never to be delivered) for the Karanga king. Four years later Francisco Barreto left for the Monomotapa gold mines, only to be thwarted by local tribes. In 1573, a second expedition wiped out Muslim traders at Sena and erected earth-walled forts at Tete and Sena. This extension of Portuguese control enabled them to subjugate most of the Karanga chieftancies by the mid-18th century.

RISE OF THE MONOMOTAPA

In the history of east-central Africa two names stand out: Great Zimbabwe (centred on the stone citadel at present-day Masvingo in Zimbabwe) and Monomotapa (a grouping of Karanga chieftaincies). In the late 15th century, the decline of Great Zimbabwe, for a thousand years a centre of trade and religion, was paralleled by the rise of the Monomotapa. During this time, dominant Zimbabwe families moved north, but stone ruins at Manekweni, north of Inhambane, prove that sections of the Karanga elite moved southeastwards.

The *Prazo* Problem

Until they were outlawed in the 1930s, the *prazos de coroa* (leased crown estates) were one of Mozambique's most fascinating features. They were not introduced to deprive the indigenous people of their land, but evolved when white renegades established niches for themselves within African society, often

Above: *The 16th-century fortress of São Sebastião on Mozambique Island provided refuge for the islanders during raids by Betsimisaraka slavers.*

through marriage. The *prazo* communities produced new cultural and social practices which reflected their Afro–Asian–European mix.

The Portuguese crown granted land to religious orders, noblemen and discharged soldiers who often recruited private armies to extract further concessions from local chiefs. By 1670, *muzungo* (Afro-Portuguese) warlords had extorted most of northern **Karangaland** for themselves. Predictably, this lawlessness prevented the development and taxation of the region, thus becoming a major headache for the Portuguese administration. The government offered to recognize land claims on condition that *prazo* holders kept order, maintained roads, provided soldiers and paid for the upkeep of government buildings. In an attempt to increase the number of European women in Mozambique, *prazo* concessions were granted to orphaned girls and widows. Since women were often left widowed several times, some managed to accumulate vast tracts of land by way of a succession of marriages.

Slaves, Pirates and the Scramble for Africa

In 1808 a fleet of war canoes appeared along the northern Mozambique coast, the biggest of several assembled by **Betsimisaraka** chiefs from Madagascar between 1800 and 1820, in search of slaves. The ferocity of the invaders partially depopulated the coast from Kilwa (Tanzania) to

MARECHAL
SAMORA MOISES MACHEL

LOURENÇO MARQUES

Although a Portuguese trader named Lourenço Marques had sailed into this 'bay of the lagoon' (now Maputo Bay) in 1544, the site of present-day **Maputo** (formerly Lourenço Marques) consisted of little more than makeshift dwellings around the Fortaleza da Nossa Senhora da Conceição.
As the safest natural harbour between Cape Town and Mozambique Island, the bay became the focus of British expansion from the south. The resulting territorial dispute between **Britain** and **Portugal** was eventually arbitrarily settled in favour of Portugal by French president, **Marie Edme Macmahon**. Lourenço Marques developed swiftly, and only 25 years later inherited the status of capital from Mozambique Island.

Mozambique Island. In 1816 the Afro-Portuguese on Ibo retreated to the protection of the fort and successfully repelled the pirates. These attacks decimated communities which had themselves lived off slave trade for centuries.

The east African barter in slaves accelerated when France, expanding sugar plantations on its Indian Ocean possessions, needed extra labour. Despite having banned other European powers from trading on the Mozambican coast, the Portuguese quickly instituted large-scale slaving, receiving foodstuffs and silver in return. By 1775 the French were exporting about 1500 slaves a year from Ibo and Mozambique islands. When the Napoleonic Wars disrupted the slave trade between West Africa and America and buyers looked to Mozambique, which exported 30,000 souls in 1828.

In 1875 the Portuguese abolished slavery and *prazos*, attempting to replace them with citizenship, legal rights and the duty to pay taxes and do military service. During the 1884 **Berlin Congress**, Britain contested Portugal's presence in Mozambique, insisting that effective occupation was the only acceptable basis for territorial claims. When **Cecil J Rhodes**' British South Africa Company officially claimed free navigation of the Zambezi, Portugal countered by sending two steam gunships upriver to protect Massingire. The British demanded their retreat and issued orders to mobilize their own fleet. The Portuguese capitulated in January 1890, and although some wrangling followed, Mozambique's borders have changed little since then.

Greater Autonomy and World War I

Mozambique Island lost its capital status to the southern port of **Lourenço Marques** in 1902 due to the increased economic links with South Africa. Despite Lisbon giving increased autonomy to Mozambique in the 1920s, Portugal-oriented administrators continued to rule the colony, excluding the settlers and Afro-Portuguese from power. During the closing stages of **World War I** Portugal joined the winning side to secure its colonial possessions. In 1926 a military coup overthrew the government of Portugal and by 1930 a professor of finance, **Antonio Salazar**, began to take control of the country's affairs, creating a closed economic system with the colonies. The **Colonial Act** of 1933 made Mozambique part of the Portuguese state with a common law and centrally planned economy.

From Liberation Struggle to Democracy

After World War II, awakening **African nationalism** began to challenge the colonial powers. Portuguese attempts to isolate Mozambique from this trend were thwarted by returning migrant labourers who had been exposed to liberation politics. **Manu**, an early Mozambican independence movement, gathered in 1960 to petition the Portuguese administrator in Mueda, but troops ended the demonstration by shooting dozens of civilians. Atrocities like this helped to politicize Mozambicans and **Frelimo** (Mozambican Liberation Front) was formed in Dar es Salaam in 1962. Frelimo's armed wing, the FPLM (Popular Mozambique Liberation Forces), launched its **armed struggle** with an attack on Chai in northern Mozambique on 25 September 1964. Initially, Frelimo's campaign was unsuccessful, but after the assassination of leader Eduardo Mondlane in 1969, new commandant, **Samora Machel**, mounted attacks as far south as Tete and Manica. Meanwhile the Portuguese had been diverting investment from Mozambique to the EEC (European Economic Community). When the April 1974 revolution brought a new anti-colonial regime to power in Portugal, Mozambican soldiers defected, political prisoners were released and the governor general recalled to Lisbon. Chaos ensued and white settlers fled to **South Africa** in their thousands. On 25 June 1975 Mozambique gained independence, Portugal recognizing the

> **RESISTANCE TO PORTUGUESE RULE**
>
> In 1960, Tanzania declared itself a Marxist State and, as Mozambique's northern neighbour, began to provide bases for Makonde exiles who had crossed the Rovuma River after being deprived of their land by commercial Portuguese farmers. Initial half-hearted guerilla incursions had little impact on the white settlers who responded by calling a meeting with Makonde chiefs which was held at Mueda in Cabo Delgado during 1964. There are conflicting reports, but confusion ensued when discussions became heated. The Portuguese commandos opened fire, killing many of the Makonde leaders. Outrage fuelled internal resistance and greater Soviet intervention in Mozambique.

Opposite: *A statue of the former president, Samora Machel, in Maputo.*
Below: *Samora Machel in battle fatigues – a mural near Maputo's airport.*

Opposite: *Maputo street scene showing the red-roofed Banco Commercial building.*

Frelimo government without insisting on elections. Shortly afterwards almost all skilled administrators and workers had departed, leaving behind Frelimo personnel who adopted (often disastrous) policies rooted in Marxist theory, rather than on any knowledge of the job at hand.

Civil War and the New Mozambique

In 1977 the government of **Rhodesia** (now Zimbabwe) secretly formed the rebel **Renamo** (Mozambique National Resistance) movement to destroy transport and communication links. From 1977 until 1992 Mozambique was devastated by a civil war which destroyed the social and economic fabric of the entire nation. During this period Frelimo experienced many difficulties in trying to govern Mozambique. After Zimbabwe's independence in 1980 and its withdrawal of support, South Africa backed Renamo which sought external credibility as an anti-communist movement. In 1984, presidents **Botha** of South Africa and **Machel** of Mozambique signed the **Nkomati Accord**, agreeing not to support armed insurrection in each other's countries. Machel travelled abroad, shunning his Marxist backers by visiting Britain and Portugal, a campaign cut short by the 1986 air-crash which tragically ended his life. It was left to Joaquim Chissano to bring Renamo to heel.

At its third congress (1990), in keeping with world trends, Frelimo formally departed from its disastrous **Marxist–Leninist** ideology, while the collapse of the Soviet Union hastened the Russian departure. Renamo rebels continued to sabotage the infrastructure until a **cease-fire** agreement was signed on 15 October 1992. UN-supervised democratic multi-party elections were held in 1994. Mozambique's reconstruction progressed quickly. Truce paved the way for the deployment of a UN peace-keeping force (Onumoz) which immediately set about facilitating the disarmament of all armed groups. In the face of a sceptical world, Frelimo and Renamo laid down arms and began campaigning in the political arena.

Finally, in 1997, the reopening of Gorongosa National Park, past Renamo headquarters, symbolized a peaceful and prosperous new era for the country.

SOVIET MOZAMBIQUE

During the Cold War the former Soviet Union exported its brand of international Marxism to Africa. By 1958 Mozambican guerillas trained by Russian advisers were launching small-scale raids from Tanzania. Unexpectedly, a socialist revolution in Portugal toppled the Portuguese government in 1975 and Mozambique was literally handed over to Frelimo. Not ready to govern, Frelimo persecuted the white Mozambicans who left in droves. Russian advisers arrived to fill the vacuum. Insulating themselves from the locals, they pillaged natural resources like wildlife, forests and seafood. By the time the Soviets left, after the collapse of communism in 1990, few Mozambicans lamented and even fewer could claim to have benefited from their presence.

GOVERNMENT AND ECONOMY
The New Mozambique

The new Mozambique must certainly count as one of the shining success stories of the worldwide UN peace-keeping operations.

South Africa's political transformation, combined with the determination of a people tired of violence as well as the efforts of aid groups, laid the foundation for Mozambique's highly successful and peaceful November 1994 elections. Today Frelimo may still be the ruling party, but Mozambique is unrecognizable from the days when running water was a luxury, and travellers risked their lives simply by leaving the relative safety of the cities. The government is encouraging development through tourism. Former state-owned enterprises have been privatized, placing them on a sound commercial footing. Freedom of the press is being respected and local daily newspapers present lively, critical debate on issues of the day.

The combination of a friendly people determined to progress, sound governance and an exciting natural environment being opened up to visitors, certainly demonstrate that Mozambique has a very positive future indeed.

TOWERS OF IVORY

Elephant tusks were a much-coveted resource, ruthlessly exploited by the Arabs, the Portuguese and Renamo. 18th- and 19th-century reports speak of boats capsizing under the weight of the tusks while transferring them to bigger ships. Although hunters decimated Mozambique's elephants before sanctuaries such as Gorongosa were proclaimed, it took a civil war to finally silence the great beasts. Mozambique's elephant population was reduced from a proud 20,000 to a few hundred by 1990. Both Renamo rebels and the Frelimo government sold or bartered ivory for weapons. Perhaps it is not surprising that South Africa's 1984 commitment to cease its support of the Renamo movement coincided with the first effective worldwide ban on the ivory trade.

Right: *Many containers are lined up in Maputo's busy harbour.*
Opposite: *A busy through route – the Nyamapanda border post into Zimbabwe.*

Economic Reconstruction

For hundreds of years Mozambique was administered from Portugal and therefore its economical infrastructure was aimed primarily at facilitating the **export** of agricultural and mineral products to the mother country. Although Mozambique was still reasonably prosperous in 1975, 95% of the indigenous population was illiterate and only a small handful possessed any formal qualifications or skills.

After the Portuguese withdrew, a transitional government was formed by Frelimo in 1974, and **Joaquim Chissano** took control. The following year **Samora Machel** became leader of Frelimo, and thus the first president of an independent Mozambique, which he declared a one-party Marxist state.

Not surprisingly, the country's economy slipped into almost total chaos as essential services literally ceased to exist. Soviet and East German troops and advisers, who were invited by Samora Machel to fill the void, managed to contribute very little and the economy continued to decline rapidly. In addition, support for Rhodesian and South African liberation movements cost Mozambique dearly and destroyed its last hope for progress.

DUSTING OFF DEMOCRACY

Whether or not democracy can be maintained remains to be seen. A look at the issues which have dominated discussion in the fledgling parliament is enlightening. Initially Renamo didn't bother to take up its seats but when the question of salary scales for members of parliament came up for discussion, the hall was packed and lively debate continued forthwith. Landmines that were laid during the civil war may continue to claim innocent victims for years to come but at least there is accord over one important issue: parliamentarians feel they deserve higher salaries.

When President Machel died in a plane crash in 1986, the country had descended into profound chaos, and it was up to his successor, Joaquim Chissano, to rescue the situation and transform the economy into a **free market system**.

Rebuilding Mozambique's Roads

Reduced to perilous strips of pot-holed tarmac by years of neglect and sabotage, Mozambique's roads have been one of the first of the essential services to receive the government's much-needed attention.

The resurfacing of a strategic 1700km (1056-mile) stretch of the **EN1**, the national road between **Maputo** and **Beira**, has been completed. Most other main routes south of the Zambezi are in satisfactory condition. A four-lane toll road on a more direct route between **Ressano Garcia** (Komatipoort in South Africa) and Maputo is under construction as is a brand-new road to the north which bypasses Maputo, via Moamba, Magude and Macia. The recommended road to Maputo from South Africa is the abovementioned Komatipoort/Ressano Garcia route as it is in good condition.

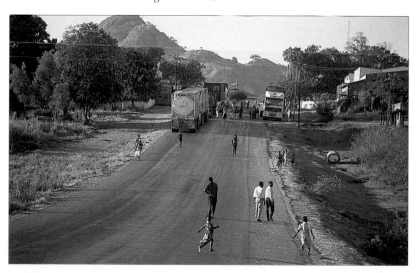

PEACE AT LAST

Mozambique today is a nation undergoing a fundamental economic and social transformation. The media are no longer censored and freedom of movement is guaranteed under the new constitution. International investors and entrepreneurs are renovating the old lodges and hotels and building new ones. Even in the most remote regions, schools and hospitals have either been rebuilt or are under construction. Buses, trucks and taxis are once more transporting people throughout the country. Since the momentous peace accord of October 1992, Mozambicans are fast regaining a reputation for being among the friendliest in the world.

Agriculture

Prior to 1975 **copra** (dried coconut flesh) formed one of Mozambique's most important exports. In 1979, copra formed 10% of the country's agricultural production. The extracted oils were extensively used by the international cosmetic industry. The main coconut-producing areas are along the coastal plains of the Inhambane, Zambezia and Nampula provinces.

Since coconut plantations are located in coastal areas, copra production is affected by the periodic cyclones that uproot trees and rip unripe fruit from the branches. On the Island of Querimba north of Pemba, the Gessner family has cultivated coconuts for three generations and although cyclone Demoina damaged thousands of trees, their gigantic estate of some 40,000 trees was the only one able to function throughout the civil war. Those of us with no use for either copra or coconut husks will be pleased to know that there are other ways to enjoy this delectable fruit. Young green coconuts, known to the locals as *lanhos*, which are full of refreshing pure **coconut water**, are sold on the roadside wherever the palms grow. For a handful of currency, the *lanho* of your choice will have its top lopped off and you will be able to slake the most urgent of thirsts on up to a litre of the delicately sweet fluid – also distilled into a lethal liquor called *sura*.

In 1973, Mozambique exported 125,000 tonnes of **cashew nuts**, the country's largest food export at the time. Although by 1983 this had been reduced to a few

Left: *Fishing is an important source of income for many Mozambicans.*
Opposite: *Cashew nuts are processed and packed at this factory in Monapo.*

rotting sackloads, it is still the best (and cheapest) country for properly dried and processed cashew nuts.

The occurrence of **prawns** along the Mozambique coast generally coincides with the location of mangrove swamps. The decline of the prawn population, particularly in Maputo Bay, can be ascribed to the destruction of the mangroves at the Maputo and Incomáti river mouths. In 1983, the combined catch of commercial and subsistence prawn fishermen was in the region of 10,000 tonnes, the majority of the prawns originating from the nutrient-rich waters off Maputo, Sofala and Nampula provinces.

Marine Resources

Pelagic fish such as anchovy, barracuda and sardine are found throughout the shallow coastal waters at the fringe of the broad Mozambique Channel. In deeper waters tuna, marlin and sailfish occur, the St Lazarus Bank east of Moçímboa da Praia being one of the few places in the world where marlin are known to breed. Rising long before dawn, subsistence fishermen still enact an ancient ritual unifying man and sea as they sail their bamboo platforms towards the horizon. By mid-morning they return laden with fish – if the gods have been kind.

Commercial trawlers come from afar to exploit these riches and this area of the ocean is not exempt from the worldwide problem of ruthless overfishing.

AN EMBATTLED ECONOMY

Prior to 1980 Mozambique's main exports were cashew nuts, petroleum derivatives, prawns, tea, sugar and cotton. The Gross Domestic Product (GDP) was made up of 50% agriculture, 40% industry, 5% transport and communications with the balance contributed by commerce and administration. However, such was the extent of Mozambique's economic decline that, between the years 1973 to 1983, the country ceased to be able to feed its citizens, having to rely on shipments of foreign food aid instead. Only the air transport industry prospered due to the frequent ambushes on the roads and railways. Millions of Mozambican peasants fled into neighbouring countries where they lived in refugee camps until 1994.

Right: *The Cahora Bassa dam fills a beautiful valley.*
Opposite: *A woman of the Makua tribe, one of Mozambique's eight main tribal groups.*

The End of the Work

The name **Cahora Bassa** (Cabora Bassa in colonial times) is probably a corruption of the Chewa term *kebrabassa*, their name for the once magnificent stretch of rapids in the gorge across which the dam was constructed. *Kebrabassa* means 'the end of the work', an appropriate name for the point where traders and travellers, who were using the Zambezi as a route into the interior, were forced to turn back by the rocks and waterfalls. Boats paddled by locally 'recruited' slaves found their progress blocked at Kebrabassa (now Songo), and explorers like David Livingstone, who was searching for a navigable route into central Africa, could only drift back downstream to Tete, probably to the considerable relief of the pitifully treated serfs.

Although Cahora Bassa was a joint venture between South Africa, Portugal and the province of Mozambique, energy transmission along the direct current lines to South Africa was cut in 1986 when **Renamo** rebels sabotaged pylons in response to the termination of their South African support in terms of the **Nkomati Accord**.

At present no power from Cahora Bassa reaches South Africa but a US$150 million plan, to de-mine the pylon servitude and repair the lines, is already out to tender. Until work is complete, southern Mozambique will have to continue to rely on South Africa's Electrical Supply Commission (ESCOM).

CAHORA BASSA HYDRO-ELECTRIC PROJECT

- Date of completion: 1974.
- Dam type: double-curved concrete arch.
- Dam height: 160m (525ft).
- Dam wall height: 331m (1086ft).
- Length: 270km (168 miles).
- Capacity: 52,000 million m³.
- Average inflow: 2800 cumecs (98,881 cusecs).
- Flood inflow: over 30,000 cubic metres per second.
- Area: 2660km² (1027 sq miles).
- Catchment area: 1,200,000 km² (463,200 sq miles).
- Generating potential: 4000 megawatt.
- Length of Direct Current (DC) transmission lines: (Songo–Apollo near Pretoria), 2400km (1491 miles).
- Length of AC transmission lines: (Songo–Chimoio and Songo–Nampula) 2000km (1243 miles).

THE PEOPLE

Of the eight major tribal groups resident in Mozambique, the Tsonga dominate the south, the Shona and Zambezi Valley tribes (Chuabo, Sena, Nyungwe) the central region, and the Yao and Makua–Lómwè are dominant in the north.

The 1820 Mfecane wars unleashed by Shaka, Zululand's (South Africa) warrior king, generated violent waves of unrest which uprooted hundreds of thousands of people, and reached as far north as Kenya. Small groups of Nguni fled into Mozambique, but scattered on coming into contact with resident tribes to avoid being viewed as a threat. Remnants of the Nguni still cling to the fringes of the Lebombo Mountains near Namaacha, at the confluence of the Limpopo and Shangane rivers, at Espungabera at the headwaters of the Buzi River and on the Angónia Plateau in northern Tete province. Due to its unsuitability for cattle (tsetse fly is rife), Mozambique was, for the most part, spared the destruction by Shaka.

The Makonde tribe of northern Cabo Delgado and southern Tanzania had their own reputation for territorial aggression. They had always been staunchly independent, resisting incursions first from the Arabs, and later from the Portuguese. The liberation struggle in Mozambique started with Makonde herders being forcefully evicted from their land by Portuguese farmers, a move bound to end in bloodshed.

Language

Of the 17 more important **ethnic languages** spoken in Mozambique, the most common are, in the south: Shangaan, Tswa and Ronga; in the central region: Shona, Sena and Nyanja; while to the north the main vernaculars are: Makua, Lómwè, Chuabo, Yao and Makonde.

TRIBAL DIFFERENCES

An interesting tribal divide, closely following the course of the Zambezi, is that the northern tribes are uniformly matriarchal, while those in the south are almost entirely patriarchal. However, the tribes of the Zambezi valley itself, as well as those influenced by the patriarchal Islamic religion along the far northern coast, contradict this pattern. From Pemba northwards, a distinctive language called Makua has developed, which is only vaguely related to the surrounding languages. Only a short distance inland from the coast, Makua gives way quite abruptly to Lómwè and Makonde.

BASIC SHANGAAN

Good day • *Absheni*
How are you? • *Minjani?*
I am fine • *Nikhona*
What is this place?
• *Iyini ndawu leyi?*
Where is . . .?
• *Yikwini . . .?*
How much is that?
• *Imalumuni?*
What is your name?
• *Imani bito rawena?*
Thank you • *Nakhensa*
May I take your photograph?
• *Ni nga teka shitombe?*
Where does this road go to?
• *Ndlola loyi yiyakwini?*
What is the name of this in
Shangaan? • *Iyini bito
rashileshi hishi shangaan?*

Opposite: *On Mozambique
Island the influence of past
Arab traders is tangible.*
Below: *This Catholic church
on Ibo Island is said to date
back to the 16th century.*

Portuguese was and still is the everyday language of
commerce and technology – even the Frelimo government
declared Portuguese to be the country's official language.
A survey undertaken in 1980 revealed that only about 25%
of the total urban population could speak Portuguese, with
about half this number applicable in the rural areas. Only
10% of Maputo's citizens spoke Portuguese at home, while
the proportion of Mozambican citizens who grew up
speaking Portuguese was less than 2%. **English** may not
easily be understood away from upmarket hotels, lodges
and restaurants, but if a street urchin in Beira or Maputo
suddenly berates you in perfect English for not giving him
or her money, don't be surprised. Many of Mozambique's
children who are under the age of 12 grew up in refugee
camps in one of the English-speaking countries surrounding Mozambique. **Funakalo**, the discredited language
once spoken mainly by South Africa's black miners,
remains a valuable communication medium. However,
a few phrases of **Shangaan** will elicit more smiles.

Religion

During Mozambique's Marxist period, organized religion was suppressed by the Frelimo government, thus
no accurate statistics have been kept for this period.

Presently, the urbanized population has adopted **Catholicism**, most common in the south, while further north Islam becomes more dominant. Traditional practices such as **ancestor worship** and **animism** are still widespread. This was used to profound effect by the protagonists who influenced the Mozambicans both during the period of conflict as well as prior to the 1994 general election.

Traditional Cultures

With a coastline settled by adventurers from Arabia and southern Europe as well as diverse wandering African tribes, Mozambique is unique in southern and eastern Africa. Although geographically part of southern Africa, this former **Portuguese** colony has a historical and cultural heritage more closely related to **Muslim** northeast Africa, but its population also exhibits a lively, Latin outlook on life.

Whether you enter the country from Malawi, Tanzania (Rovuma crossing by dugout only), Zambia, Zimbabwe, South Africa or Swaziland, by boat via one of the many harbours or by air into Maputo International Airport, you will be faced with the challenge of communicating with people whose command of the **English** language is weak.

Most popular tourist destinations lie along the coast where people live in small fishing villages, and dhows are the main means of transport. From basic meeting places under trees in mud-and-straw 'suburbs' to chic nightclubs in the cities, the music that is belted out everywhere ranges from sensuous **samba**, **salsa** and **rumba** to thrilling **tango**.

PASSION IN PEMBA

A night of *enika* (spirit distilled from pineapples), swaying hips and beautiful 'mulatto' girls with wild shining eyes, under the palms of Pemba's *bairro* (informal suburb) of Paquete-Quete is the stirring stuff of a Bob Dylan ballad. Mozambique is a refreshingly unusual country embracing a cultural mix that resembles a cross between Brazil, India, Arabia and Africa, a welcome contrast to the surrounding English-speaking African states. By Western standards, Mozambique remains desperately poor – yet its people are proud, courteous and very mindful of good manners.

Right: *Murals such as this one in a park in Tete, often commemorate the years of the liberation struggle.*
Opposite: *Many tourists come to lovely Benguerra Island to fly fish.*

MOZAMBICAN MASTERS

Malangatana, artistic ambassador of Mozambique, has turned his hand to painting, drawing, engraving, ceramics, tapestry design, sculpture, and murals. Born of peasant parents near Matola in 1936, he herded animals, attended a Catholic school and worked as a servant, before discovering art. A year spent in a colonial jail (1970) curtailed his creativity and after 1975, politics consumed his passion. Malangatana took up painting once more in 1981 with his trademark of fiery, naked, disembodied figures cavorting with mythical beasts.

Chissano started carving at the age of 29. He had no formal education and worked on the South African gold mines. During a job as cleaner at an artistic association, he tried his own hand at carving. Chissano held his first one-man exhibition in Lourenço Marques (Maputo) in 1964. All his works are untitled, but characteristically follow the natural grain and shape of each chunk of wood. Chissano died in Matola in 1994. Both Malangatana and Chissano's work is on display at Maputo's National Art Museum (*see* p.38).

Mozambique's Art World

In the 1950s some of the European painters belonging to Lourenço Marque's art nucleus began to feel the challenging burden of living on a continent rich in unrecognized indigenous art forms. Moving away from Eurocentrism, they started addressing local social themes, using visual motifs observed in popular tradition to create works more identifiably 'Mozambican'. Today, big beaming round faces and large white eyes are evidently the way Mozambicans see themselves when turning their hands to painting murals.

By independence in 1975, the liberation movements began to promote local culture. A cultural centre was formed to nurture local art. Most new artists initially imitated the predominant personalities in Mozambique's plastic arts. During the 1975–85 period, due to civil turmoil, their imagery dealt mainly with the immediacy of political militancy.

The Mozambican artists' geographical isolation, lack of training and the absence of a formal art trade had an unexpected consequence: a large number of painters were able to make a living by personally marketing and selling their own work. Without the discipline and attention to style demanded by classical art academies, a freshness of style and lack of inhibition was preserved in Mozambique, characteristic of what may be termed the 'Mozambican school'.

Theatre

Maputo's Teatro Avenida on Avenida 25 de Setembro
sometimes hosts stage productions. Mozambique's
Compania de Art, Canto e Dans, based in the Rua
de Bagamoio (opposite Luso), also occasionally puts
on shows depicting various traditional dance styles.
See the daily newspaper, *Noticias*, for details.

Sport and Recreation

Mozambique's most popular sports are **basketball,
soccer** (football) and **athletics**. Maputo's **Maria Mutola**
holds the world record for the women's 800m track race.
Basketball, particularly, has thrived and the national
team has been African champion for many years. Indoor
basketball courts are located in most of the main cities
and towns, with the club in steamy Quelimane being
particularly competitive. Golfers can only play a round
in Maputo, where one of the accepted obstacles at the
Campo de Golfe de Maputo, a little inland from Costa
do Sol, are fairways lined with tin shanties, and people
doing their laundry in the water hazards. The local
population of Morrungulo is threatening to install a
few greens, among the palms and between the dunes.

ART AND ARCHITECTURE

Makonde: in a remote area
straddling the Mozambique/
Tanzania border, the Makonde
tribe's sculptures depict a
bizarre mixture of ancestor
worship and Christianity.
Malangatana: this celebrated painter used disturbing
surreal images of violence to
publicize the horrors of war.
Manueline: ornate style of
architecture popular during
the reign of King Emanuel I
of Portugal. He transformed
Portugal into a maritime
power and his reign is considered to be the most brilliant
in the country's history. The
Natural History Museum
in Maputo was built in
the Manueline style.
Art Deco: architectural form
resulting from the combination of traditional and modern
approaches. Maputo has
some fine examples along
the Avenida Samora Machel.

Food and Drink

A continental characteristic which has remained firmly entrenched in the larger Mozambican towns such as Maputo, Beira and Quelimane is the love of wine, company and song. The Portuguese standard here is: *entradas* (entrées) of *prego* (steak roll), *chouriço* (spicy sausage), *rissois* (shrimps in batter) and *sopa de mariscos* (shellfish soup) followed by a main dish of perhaps *lulas grelhado* (grilled calamari), *espetada* (kebab), *galinha inteiro com piri-piri* (whole chicken piri-piri), *peixe cozido com todos* (boiled fish, usually cod, with rice or potato chips, and tomato salad) or perhaps *caranguejo recheado* (stuffed crab). Top it all with a *pudim* (pudding) of *gelado sorvete* (ice cream sorbet) and *salada de frutas* (fruit salad).

Since Mozambique's climate ranges from tropical to temperate and from arid to very humid, indigenous and cultivated fruit and vegetables available are rich

in variety. Rainfall, generally speaking, increases from south to north, decreasing from east to west, and so does the availability and assortment of food. Fresh Portuguese-style bread rolls (*pãozinho*), often baked in hollowed-out ant hills (*termitaria*), are widely available throughout the country, even in the most isolated places. As long as you have something to smear on that hot loaf, you need never go hungry.

To savour the delicious assortment of Mozambican fruit and vegetables at its best, it is necessary to take the effect of seasonal influences into account. Nicuadala near Quelimane may produce some of the world's largest, juiciest and sweetest **pineapples**,

Left: *A Chimoio woman, her baby tied securely on her back, sifts maize meal.*
Opposite: *A barbecue on Magaruque Island consists of delicious crayfish tails.*

while the **papaya** at Pemba is surely worth the airfare on LAM from Maputo. But if you arrive in August (winter in Mozambique), both these delicious crops will be in extreme short supply and you will have to settle for bananas, tomatoes and green vegetables. Of course, along the coast there is always **seafood**, while inland the staple diet is *mandioca* (**cassava**) and **corn porridge**.

If you are cooking for yourself and intend shopping at the markets, carry a small fisherman's scale, as well as your own selection of condiments and herbs. Even if you intend eating out, most restaurants do not offer a decent selection of condiments, so it is always wise to carry salt and pepper cellars, lemon juice and whatever sauces you can't live without.

Note that the **service** in restaurants (where it exists at all) is usually painfully **slow**, almost comically so. Your well-meaning waiter may consider two hours a reasonable preparation time for your meal, and would feel mortally insulted by complaints about the delay, or the cold food.

MOZAMBICAN DELIGHTS

Matata (shrimp and peanut stew) is a typical local mainstay. Imagine a combination of shrimps, peanuts, crushed coconut and tender, young spinach. Chopped red pepper is optional.
Frango a Cafriál (barbecued chicken) is a plump chicken rubbed down with hot piri-piri sauce and roasted over an open charcoal brazier.
Sopa de Feijão Verde (green bean soup) has fresh green beans cut across in thin slices, boiled and served in a thin tomato and onion purée.
Salada de Pera Abacate (avocado salad) is served on a bed of crisp lettuce, doused with a herb, olive oil and lemon dressing.
Ananas con Vinho do Porto (fresh pineapple in Port): a little sugar, some crushed, roasted cashew nuts and, of course, a helping of Port, liberally sprinkled on the fruit.

2
Maputo

This important southern Indian Ocean port lies less than 100km (60 miles) from neighbouring Swaziland and South Africa. With its subtropical climate, beautiful sheltered bay and blend of Portuguese architecture, African spontaneity and Indian cuisine, Maputo (formerly Lourenço Marques) has retained much of its colonial mystique. Nightclubs swing to samba rhythms until dawn and a host of *quiosques* (kiosks) serve *galinha piri-piri* (chicken piri-piri), *matapas* (a delicious cassava-leaf dish), *bacalhau* (dried cod) and some of the best *batata frita* (fried potato chips) in the world. Hundreds of *salões* (sidewalk cafés), dozens of nightclubs and the odd sleazy strip-joint complement the vibrant atmosphere of this capital city which feels more Latin-American than African.

Modelled on Portuguese harbour cities such as Lisbon and Porto, Maputo's wide avenues are lined with pavements inlaid with attractive black-and-white stone mosaics. Laid out in a grid pattern in 1847, the 'long' avenues extend at right angles to **Avenida da Marginal** while the 'short' avenues traverse Maputo Hill away from the bay. By car, you will enter the city via the large traffic circle on Av. 24 de Julho, and proceed for 5km (3 miles) before reaching Av. Julius Nyerere, the heart of the *cima*, or upper city. Visitors arriving at **Maputo International Airport** will enter the city via Av. de Acordos de Lusaka. This becomes Av. da Guerra Popular on reaching the high-rise area, runs downhill to the *baixa* – the lower city – and ends at the massive 'peace goddess' statue in the centre of the square opposite the Maputo Railway Station.

Don't Miss

*** Feira Popular: funfair complex with over 30 pubs restaurants and nightclubs.
** Mercado Xipamanine: notorious and exotic market in Mafalala, where you really can buy anything.
** Av. da Marginal: walk along the promenade where vendors exhibit their wares.
* Catembe: take a ferry across the bay for a wonderful view of the Maputo skyline.
* Kowhana: join the locals at this nightclub in Mafalala and lambada until dawn.

Opposite: *Aerial view over Maputo's Jardim Tunduru Botanical Gardens.*

THE STREETS OF MAPUTO

As in most poor, third-world cities, parts of Maputo are home to the destitute and homeless. Street children are always on hand to guard your car or help you with parking. Yet a daylight stroll through the city centre will reveal sights ranging from tailored trees in **Jardim Tunduru Botanical Gardens** to the elegant sophistication of the **Hotel Polana**. Downtown Maputo's central market is clearly not a place to flash your wallet or video camera. Here the elite and the public mingle, as they haggle over tobacco, traditional medicine, papaya and prawns.

CHIEF MAPUTA'S CAPITAL

When the first Portuguese explorers landed on this coast nearly 500 years ago, they came into contact with an indigenous people ruled by Chief Maputa. Consequently, the area from Maputo Bay south to Lake St Lucia in South Africa's KwaZulu-Natal province was, and still is, often referred to as **Maputaland**. Mozambique's original capital for 200 years was the town of Mozambique, on a little island (now called Mozambique Island) about 1500km (932 miles) north offshore from Maputo. The Portuguese virtually ignored their little fortified settlement at Delagoa Bay (now Maputo Bay) until the British and the Boers began to show serious interest in the area. The MacMahon Award of 1873 eventually resolved the territorial dispute in Portugal's favour, resulting in a swiftly developing settlement. The Portuguese named it **Lourenço Marques** (now Maputo) and it inherited the status of capital from Mozambique Island in 1897.

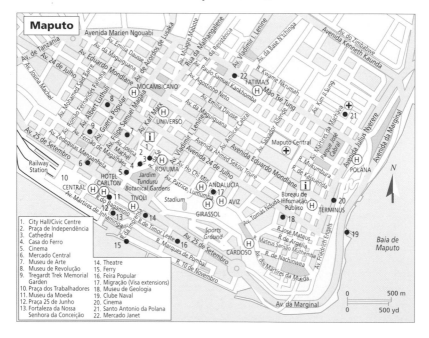

Maputo

1. City Hall/Civic Centre
2. Praça de Independência
3. Cathedral
4. Casa do Ferro
5. Cinema
6. Mercado Central
7. Museu de Arte
8. Museu de Revolução
9. Tregardt Trek Memorial Garden
10. Praça dos Trabalhadores
11. Museu da Moeda
12. Praça 25 de Junho
13. Fortaleza da Nossa Senhora da Conceição
14. Theatre
15. Ferry
16. Feira Popular
17. Migração (Visa extensions)
18. Museu de Geologia
19. Clube Naval
20. Cinema
21. Santo Antonio da Polana
22. Mercado Janet

0   500 m

0   500 yd

THE STREET OF SIN

As in all port cities, sailors (and thieves) prowl Maputo's streets at night, heading for **Rua do Bagamoio**, the so-called 'street of sin'. For a night to remember, leave your valuables behind and start at the historical **Hotel Central** on the corner of Mesquita and Bagamoio streets. Then head down Rua do Bagamoio to the **Luso** nightclub where strippers should be ready (first show at 23:00) to do justice to the area's reputation. From here, let your designated driver (or taxi) ferry you to **Feira Popular** for 'sun-uppers' from a bamboo rooftop pub overlooking the bay

Fortaleza da Nossa Senhora da Conceição *

This squat red-sandstone fortress, built between 1851–67, stands on the site of the original mud-and-pole stockade. Once a museum glorifying Portugal's colonial conquests, it is now the **State Historical Archive** and houses the remains of **Ngungunhane**, last great chief of the **Nguni** tribe, who ruled the Gaza region until British and Portuguese expansion lead to friction. He was captured and paraded through the streets of Lisbon before dying in exile in the Azores.

Historic City Sites **

In the *baixa* of Maputo, which is in fact drained swampland, many colonial buildings still stand along the Rua do Bagamoio. There is the **Hotel Central** and the dilapidated **Hotel Carlton**. The **Museu da Moeda** (Currency Museum) near the end of Rua do Bagamoio is Maputo's oldest intact example of Moorish architecture and has been beautifully restored to its original state. Open Tuesday to Thursday, and Saturday.

In an attempt to escape the mosquitoes and humidity of the *baixa*, Maputo's first hospital was erected on an (originally) densely forested hill, in an area which is now characterized by high-rise residential developments. The attractive two-storey Victorian **Central Hospital** has since been converted and is today known as **Restaurante 1908**. The city's hospital moved to larger premises next door.

Above: *Maputo's skyline as seen from the harbour.*
Below: *This wall motif in the Hotel Central displays a group of musicians.*

MAPUTO'S MAGICAL MARKETS

- **Mercado Central:**
On Av. 25 de Setembro; in existence for over 100 years. Frozen fish, Nampula cashews, Inhambane baskets; mind your bags and pockets.
- **Mercado Xipamanine:**
In the heart of Mafalala district. Get a local to take you to see the bizarre array of traditional medicines.
- **Mercado Artesanato:**
Toys sold on the Praça 25 de Junho every Saturday. Makonde sculptures available.
- **Mercado Janet:** Opposite the church. Best selection of local fruit and vegetables.
- **Fish market:** Opposite the abandoned hotel on Av. da Marginal on the way to Costa do Sol. Watch out for a few fresh prawns placed on top of the rotten ones underneath.

Below: *The beautiful Catedral de Nossa Senhora da Conceição in Maputo.*

HISTORICAL AND CULTURAL WALKS

Despite Maputo's reputation for being riddled with thieves and muggers, it is fairly safe to see the sights on foot as long as you leave your valuables behind, walk in a group and return well **before sunset**. Strolling certainly beats the frustration of trying to find parking in a city where windshields, headlamps and indicator lenses are stolen, to the extent that many owners deliberately crack these in an attempt to eliminate their resale value.

To escape the sticky midday heat, the best time to walk is during the **early morning**, especially on **Saturdays** and **Sundays**. 'Maputenses' seem superstitious about exposure to the early morning sun, and so traffic should be light until around 10:00, with another quiet spell during the afternoon 'siesta' (religiously adhered to between 12:00 and 14:00). Since the two routes allow many opportunities to slake your thirst on tea, coffee, sodas or something sturdier, it's unnecessary to carry anything with you except money and maybe some toilet paper. Those who experience anxiety attacks at the thought of dirty toilets, fear not: clean ablutions are all part of the recommended two routes which are both circular, not longer than 8km (5 miles) and have safe parking at the point of departure and return (still, don't leave valuables in your vehicle).

Baixa Walk (lower city): 8km; 5 miles **

Starting and finishing on the Rua da Sé at the Hotel Rovuma (which was being renovated at the time of writing), this route takes in historic old Maputo, and includes a very cheap government ferry ride (the terminal is a 15-minute walk from the hotel) across the bay and back. The hotel is situated opposite the huge, white **Catholic Cathedral** of Nossa Senhora da Conceição off Praça da Independência. If you get lost, look for the towering, blindingly white spire of the cathedral, which is one of the city's most unmistakable landmarks.

Stand with your back to the hotel lobby, turn right and walk a short distance uphill to

Av. Ho Chi Min. Now swing left (around the back of the cathedral) to the rear of the **City Hall** and **Civic Centre** (Conselho Executivo), which was completed in 1945. For permission to enter the Civic Centre, apply at the reception off Av. Ho Chi Min.

From the front of the City Hall, walk down the stairs to the Praça da Independência, and turn right off the square

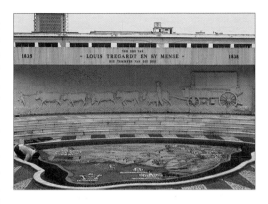

Above: *The Louis Tregardt Trek Memorial Garden commemorates the Boer pioneers' perilous journey into Mozambique.*

onto Av. Josina Machel, named after Mozambique's former first lady. Four blocks further lies the meticulously maintained **Louis Tregardt Trek Memorial Garden** which commemorates the disastrous attempts by the Transvaal Boers to secure a seaport in the 19th century. The incredible journey of the pioneers is depicted in relief on marble mosaic maps on the boundary walls, as well as on the floor of the pond.

From the monument retrace your steps along Av. Josina Machel to the circle, cross to the newly restored, original LM Club (now the **French Cultural Centre**) and walk down to **Casa do Ferro** designed by French engineer Alexandre Eiffel (*see* p. 39). Across from this prefabricated steel edifice stands the imposing statue of Samora Machel, to the side of which is the entrance to the peaceful **Jardim Tunduru Botanical Gardens**.

You are now on the wide avenue named after Samora Machel, which runs uphill from the *baixa* to the City Hall. Continue downhill to Av. 25 de Setembro (referring to the first day of the revolution) with its high-rise office blocks and shady sidewalk cafés like the **Scala** or **Café Continental**. Turn right at this intersection and continue for two blocks to the **Mercado Municipal** on your right. The market offers a maze of stalls that carry anything from fresh and frozen seafood, colourful tropical fruit and odorous traditional medicines to handicraft, cloth, curios and spices. Watch out for con artists and pickpockets.

ECHOES OF PAST GRANDEUR

Already majestic from the outside, it is the interior of the neoclassical **Civic Centre** that is really rewarding. There are magnificent crystal chandeliers, intricate tile mosaics of Portuguese ships, Louis XIV fittings and furniture. Beside the marble staircase in the reception hall are beautiful scale models of the historic buildings of old Maputo.

Leave the **Mercado Municipal** via its main entrance and cross Av. 25 de Setembro to the Rua da Mesquita. Now walk towards the docks and you will pass Maputo's first **mosque** on your left, before reaching an unmistakable landmark, the Victorian **Hotel Central** on the corner of Mesquita and Bagamoio streets. You are now right in the heart of the *baixa*, or downtown Maputo.

New York may have its Lady Liberty, but the statue that dominates Maputo's Praça dos Trabalhadores could hold a candle to it anytime. An intimidating 10m (33ft) stone statue of the Greek goddess Athena, sculpted from Portuguese granite after the Great War of 1914–18 by Rui Gameiro, is represented staring sternly towards the entrance of the railway station, sword and shield in hand. Local legend tells of a formidable woman who rid the area of a snake by boiling it in a pot of water balanced on her head.

Almost 90 years after it was constructed, Maputo's **CFM Railway Station** (Caminho de Ferro de Moçambique) looks brand-new after extensive renovations were completed in 1995. From the station, return to Hotel Central and carry on down Rua do Bagamoio past the Dance Academy on your right and the Luso nightclub on your left, towards the leafy Praça 25 de Junho (a square named in honour of Mozambique's Day of Independence). One street before the Praça you will see the big and opulent **Cinema 333**. The **Museu da Moeda** and the **Fortaleza da Nossa Senhora da Conceição** (1781) gird the Praça 25 de Junho, which hosts a wonderful craft market (**Mercado Artesanato**) on Saturday mornings. Once the museum of military history, the fortress is now being transformed into the State Historical Archive. Open 07:00–17:00 weekends only.

TRANQUIL TROPICAL GARDENS

Laid out in 1883 by celebrated English landscaper Thomas Honney, who created similar parks for the King of Greece and the Sultan of Turkey, Maputo's **Jardim Tunduru Botanical Gardens** today offer a splendid escape from the hustle and bustle of the city. Hundreds of colourful shrubs, hedges and flowering plants are shaded by towering indigenous and exotic trees. The murmur of streams and the splash of fountains complement the feeling of peace and isolation. Don't miss out on a visit to the conservatory (obtain permission at the nearby office) filled with cycads, ferns and conifers, among which statues of water nymphs hide.

From the fort stroll along Av. Mártires de Inhaminga, which runs parallel to the docks, past an open field on the left to the new **Ministry of Finance** building. Here, turn towards the bay and board the rusty **ferry** at the jetty opposite the corner of Rua da Imprensa and Av. 10 de Novembro. The ferry will take you across **Maputo Bay** to the suburb of **Catembe**, a 15-minute journey costing the price of a loaf of bread. The service begins at 06:00 and ends at 20:00, with departures approximately every hour. Vehicles can be transported at a reasonable extra charge.

In Catembe you could have lunch at the **Restaurante Diogo**, a short walk left from the ferry terminal. The chef and owner is originally from Goa, and he serves delicious, reasonably priced prawns as well as other seafood.

After taking the ferry back to Maputo, turn right along Av. 10 de Novembro which runs along the bay. After a few hundred metres turn left into Rua António Fernandes (Complexo Zambi is on the corner) and one block up walk left into the **Feira Popular** complex. Wander among the pubs, clubs and funfair rides (open in the evenings) and exit away from the bay onto Av. 25 de Setembro. Turn left and make your way back towards the central market. After one block turn right into Av. Vladimir Lenine on the corner of which stands a 33-storey building. Climb the stairs (lifts are often out of order) to the top if you are still energetic enough and wish to see the **best views of Maputo**. There is refreshment at **Café Ma Stop** on the ground floor. One block up on Av. Vladimir Lenine, keep to your left to enter the **Jardim Tunduru Botanical Gardens** and take the diagonal path up to Av. Patrice Lumumba. Diagonally opposite the former **LM Radio Station** (now Radio Moçambique Studio), the British embassy was the first in the country and is still housed in the beautiful building. Turn left, then right, back up to Hotel Rovuma for a well-deserved pot of tea.

> ### FEIRA POPULAR
>
> Known to the locals simply as Feira, this fairground is an authentic Mozambican place to party the night away. Although rides operate only over weekends, the numerous pubs, clubs, kiosks and restaurants are open nightly. They range from reasonably priced Portuguese family restaurants like popular **O'Coquero** to **Complexo Zozo** which is a strip-joint-cum-restaurant.

Opposite: *One of the many shops in Maputo's Municipal (or Central) Market.*
Below: *The mural at the former LM Radio Station, now Radio Mozambique.*

MAPUTO'S MUSEUMS

Museu de Revolução:
At 3003 Av. 24 de Julho.
Mainly exhibits of **historical
interest**; emphasis on the
struggle for independence.
Museu de Geologia: On
Av. 24 de Julho. Interesting
Manueline architecture;
collection of **precious
stones and minerals**.
Museu da Moeda: On Praça
de 25 de Junho, opposite the
Banco de Mozambique. Oldest
intact building in Maputo;
houses **currency** and **barter
items** from around the world.
Museu de Arte: On Av. Ho
Chi Min. Displays of local
paintings and **sculptures**.

Opposite: *This building
in Maputo houses the
Natural History Museum.*
Below: *The elegant lobby
of the Hotel Polana exudes
luxury and refinement.*

Cima Walk (uptown): 7km; 4 miles ★★★

This walk, starting and ending at the **Hotel Polana** (designed by renowned British architect Sir Herbert Baker), explores the newer part of Maputo, built on a hill overlooking the bay. The Polana, where there is safe parking, recalls the opulent 1920s when no expense was spared on style and luxury. It is a fascinating place to visit. The Polana's marvellous lift, with its carved hardwood panels, ornate iron railings and crystal windows, is on its own worth a visit.

Walk out of the Polana parking area, cross over Av. Julius Nyerere and to your right, across Av. Mao Tsé Tung you'll see two stately old colonial homes. The first villa is still occupied by the descendants of the original owners, while the second is now the **Ungumi Restaurant**, reputedly the finest dining establishment in town, whose patron is first lady Maria Chissano. Ask the doorman to show you the magnificent entrance hall where works by Mozambique's contemporary masters are on display.

From here, continue around the building onto the Rua Kwame Nkrumah. To the right, one block up from here is the **Church of Santo Antonio da Polana**. Do enter this serene building and admire the enormous stained-glass windows extending into the soaring spire.

At the next intersection take a left turn into Av. Mártires da Machava. After five blocks you will reach Av. Eduardo Mondlane with its four traffic lanes. On the corner to your left, is the Bureau de Informação Público (**Public Information Bureau** also known as BIP) which offers a good variety of useful and informative videos, books and magazines about Mozambique.

From here turn right along Av. Eduardo Mondlane, past the sprawling grounds of the **Central Hospital** to the lovely and unmistakable **Restaurante 1908**. This Victorian-style mansion, once the hospital of Lourenço Marques, has been converted into a restaurant which serves a variety of very good Italian dishes.

Cross Av. Eduardo Mondlane to Av. Salvador Allende and walk four blocks towards the bay. At the junction with Av.

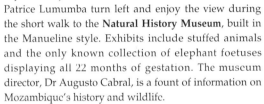

Patrice Lumumba turn left and enjoy the view during the short walk to the **Natural History Museum**, built in the Manueline style. Exhibits include stuffed animals and the only known collection of elephant foetuses displaying all 22 months of gestation. The museum director, Dr Augusto Cabral, is a fount of information on Mozambique's history and wildlife.

Walk back around the praça and turn left into Rua de Mateus Sansão Muthemba with **Clube dos Empresários** almost immediately to your left. The shady terrace overlooking the swimming pool is a great place to sit and sip a cold drink. Carry on down the road, watching out for the Associação Cultural Tchova Xitaduma on your right, two blocks before the intersection with Av. Julius Nyerere. This cultural centre often has exhibitions by local artists.

Continue with Sansão Muthemba and turn left at the junction into Av. Julius Nyerere, the road on which the Hotel Polana is situated. It is now a 2km (1¼-mile) walk back to your starting point, along a leafy avenue lined with stately homes, interesting shops and various restaurants. Pause for an ice cream, stop off for lunch, watch the passing show over a cup of espresso, and support the curio sellers who offer their wares under the trees just before you reach the parking area of the Hotel Polana.

EIFFEL'S 'HOUSE OF STEEL'

Paris may have its Eiffel Tower, but Alexandre Gustave Eiffel's fame is not restricted to France. Born in Dijon in 1832, the brilliant engineer first suggested the use of steel braces and girders to support the 485m (1600ft) Garonne bridge. This innovation was of good use to the sculptor Bartholdi, whose Statue of Liberty would otherwise probably not have been able to withstand the gales in New York Bay. Another of Eiffel's prefabricated steel structures was bolted together to form a two-storey house. The **Casa do Ferro**, next to the Jardim Tunduru Botanical Gardens, was to be the personal residence of Mozambique's governor general during 1892. However, the building proved too hot for habitation as it wasn't insulated. Today it houses the Department of Museums.

Above: *Traditional fishermen along the Incomáti River near Marracuene.*

CAFÉ SOCIETY

In Maputo, as in the cities of Portugal, most shops and businesses are closed between 12:00 and 14:00, some until 15:00, and many simply don't bother to open at all in the afternoon. Citizens while away this **siesta** period sipping espresso in the shade of one of the city's flamboyant trees (it is often too hot and humid to do anything more energetic anyway). Av. 25 de Setembro boasts many quaint cafés, such as the **Continental**, **Scala**, **Ma Stop** and **Djambu**.

AROUND MAPUTO

Mercado Xipamanine **

The history of Xipamanine market goes back to the days of Lourenço Marques and before, when black traders throughout Mozambique were restricted to the outskirts of the city limits. Adventurous tourists did, however, patronize Xipamanine, which had the reputation of selling anything from live leopards to human body parts.

Not much has changed, although today you won't find any living, wild creatures apart from the odd pet baboon. To get to Xipamanine, either take a *chapa* (taxi), or if you are driving, go out of town down Av. de Maguiguana to Praça 21 de Outobro. Turn right into Av. Angola, and then immediately left into Rua dos Imãos Roby. Carry on along this road until you arrive at the hectic, mostly open-air marketplace. Here, preferably leave someone at the car to look after it, or at least don't leave anything of value inside. Guard against pickpockets and bag-snatchers, and be sure to visit the section selling traditional medicines and talismans, where you may gain an insight into the hidden spiritual world of the Shangaan and Ronga tribes.

Xefina Grande Island **

At the end of the Marginal, a short distance out to sea, lies the larger of the two islands which guard the mouth of the Incomáti River. Although Xefina Grande is inhabited by a few traditional fishermen, the lack of fresh water has prevented extensive settlement, leaving the environment largely unspoiled. Arrange a cruise to the island through Nkomati Safaris based at the Hotel Polana. The island's **beaches** and **snorkelling** offshore are excellent. Alternatively you could explore the tumbledown ruins of the mid-16th-century Portuguese fort.

Av. da Marginal ★★★

Maputo's Marginal promenade extends from the end of Av. 25 de Setembro to the fishing village located a short distance past Restaurante Costa do Sol.

It is best to begin your promenade at the ferry jetty on Av. 10 de Novembro. Walk towards the bay mouth, pass the **Escola Nautica** (Naval School), after which you will join the Marginal, and the city's Zona Verde (green belt), at the large traffic circle. Continue under the flyover and on around the bend to the **Clube Naval** (yacht club), which was built in 1913. The club has an excellent pub, restaurant and swimming pool open to visitors on payment of a temporary membership fee. Next is **Artedif**, a workshop for disabled artisans, housed in thatched rondavels in the centre of the Marginal. Here a range of curios and leatherwork is on sale; repairs to shoes and bags are also undertaken.

Where the green belt ends, a road joins the Marginal from the left, and here reed furniture, wood carvings and colourful pottery are on sale. After this, the defunct *campismo* (caravan park), now an informal settlement, extends for about 1km (½ mile). Pubs, clubs, *quiosques* and youngsters selling ice-cold beverages from polystyrene boxes line the road all the way to **Restaurante Costa do Sol** which features a jazz band on Saturday afternoons.

KOWHANA NIGHTCLUB

With an ambience more Brazilian than African, this unique, makeshift nightclub in the heart of chaotic, densely populated Mafalala, is a must for all true 'party animals'. Rather than risk getting lost on your own, take a taxi or go with a local. Kowhana, where cabinet ministers may often be spotted, only opens on Fridays and Saturdays. In keeping with most nightclubs throughout the country, don't expect much action until after 23:00.

Below: *Lovely traditional arts and crafts are for sale along the Av. da Marginal.*

Maputo at a Glance

BEST TIMES TO VISIT

Although slightly south of the **Tropic of Capricorn**, Maputo's location along the warm Indian Ocean produces a **tropical climate**. **May** to **August** are the **driest**, **coolest** months – average temperatures around 20°C (68°F); monthly rainfall less than 30mm (1in). **October** and **November** are the **hottest**, while **December** and **January** are the **wettest**, with average monthly rainfalls of 150mm (6in).

GETTING THERE

Direct flights from Paris, Lisbon, Johannesburg, Harare, Manzini, as well as from Mozambique's provincial capitals (except Inhambane) service **Maputo International Airport**, 8km (5 miles) from the Civic Centre, tel: (1) 46-5074.
The **Mozambican airline, LAM** (Linhas Areas de Moçambique), tel: (1) 42-6001, fax: 46-5134, has regular domestic flights to Beira, Tete, Pemba, Quelimane, Nampula, and Lichinga.
You can reach Maputo from South Africa via the resurfaced Komatipoort/Ressano Garcia **road**; or from Swaziland via the good-condition Lomahasha/Namaacha route.
The **Komati Train** from Johannesburg, tel: (2711) 773-2944 (or book at Maputo Station in person), departs Johannesburg on Sunday, Tuesday and Thursday at 17:45, arriving in Maputo at 12:00 the following day.

The **Panthera Azul** luxury **buses** do the trip every day; Maputo, tel: (1) 49-3025; or tel: (2711) 337-7409, Johannesburg, South Africa.

GETTING AROUND

Maputo International Airport is served by city **taxis**, but always negotiate the entire fare, before you take the ride. **Travel agents** will transfer you to your hotel by prior arrangement. Around town, locals use *chapas* ranging from mini-buses to trucks.
Car-hire firms:
Hertz, tel: (1) 49-1003, fax: 42-6077.
Avis, tel: (1) 46-5140, fax: 46-5493.
Air charter companies:
Sabin Air, tel: (1) 46-5108, Natair, tel: (1) 49-1811, fax: 49-1872.
Long-distance buses:
Transportes Oliveiras, terminus just after the circle at the end of Av. 24 de Julho tel: (1) 73-2108.
Transportes Virginia (north to Beira), based at Hotel Universo, tel: (1) 42-2225 or 42-7003.

WHERE TO STAY

Cima (Uptown)
LUXURY
(Payment in US$.)
Hotel Polana, 1380 Av. Julius Nyerere, tel: (1) 49-1001/1, fax: 49-1480. One of Africa's truly gracious hotels. Stunning views, swimming pool and tropical garden.

Hotel Cardoso, 707 Av. dos Mártires de Mueda, tel: (1) 49-1071/5, fax: 49-4054. Stylish, clean; incredible views of sunsets over Maputo Bay.

Terminus, 587 Francisco Orlando Magumbwe, tel: (1) 49-1333, fax: 49-1284. Comfortable and air-conditioned with satellite cable TV.

MID-RANGE
Hotel Moçambicano, 961 Av. Filipe Samuel Magaia, tel: (1) 42-9252, fax: 42-3124. Air-conditioned rooms, bar restaurant and pool.

BUDGET
Hotel Central, corner of Rua do Bagamoio and Rua da Mesquita, tel: (1) 43-1652. Historic, renovated building; with clean bathrooms; 200m (656ft) from the station, ideal for budget travellers.

Fatima's, 1317 Av. Mao Tsé Tung near Mercado Janet, tel: (1) 30-0036, fax: 49-4462. The backpacker's best bet.

Costa do Sol
MID-RANGE
The Burger Inn, *bairro de Triunfo*, tel: (1) 45-5211. Very popular, full English breakfast included in the price.

WHERE TO EAT

Seafood and **chicken** are specialities. Make sure all food is well cooked; be wary of shellfish at cheaper places.

Maputo at a Glance

Ungumi Restaurant,
1555 Av. Julius Nyerere, tel:
(1) 49-0951/11, fax: 49-1999.
Very classy; excellent French
chef; reservations essential.

Hotel Polana (*see* Where
to Stay), tel: (1) 49-1003.
A choice of three restaurants
offering excellent service.

Zé Verde, 2952 Av. Angola,
tel: (1) 46-5250. Excellent,
authentic Portuguese menu,
fado music and *vinho verde*.

Piri-Piri, 3842 Av. 24 de
Julho, tel: (1) 49-2379. Chicken
and prawns à la piri-piri.

Costa do Sol, at the end of
the Marginal, tel: (1) 45-5115,
fax: 45-5162. Delicious seafood
and a garlic-laden Greek salad.

Sheik, 67 Av. Mao Tsé Tung,
tel: (1) 49-0197. Popular
nightclub; international and
Chinese dishes; closed Sunday.

Mini-Golfe, on the Marginal,
tel: (1) 49-0382. Restaurant,
disco, swimming pool, gym
and putt-putt course.

Kowhana, out near Mercado
Xipamanine (Mafalala), tel: (1)
47-5468. The real Mozambican
thing; a little difficult to find.

Feira Popular, near the end
of Av. 25 de Setembro. Something to suit every pocket; safe
parking inside, off the Rua de
António Fernandes.

SHOPPING

Buy perishables at the local
markets. Processed goods
and luxuries are available
from **Interfranca**, 1550
Av. 24 de Julho. Various
guidebooks and maps are
obtainable at the *tabacaria*
(tobacconist shop) in the
Hotel Polana. **Artedif** on
the Marginal near Clube
Naval sells curios and traditional *capulanas* may be
bought at **Casa Elefante**,
Av. 25 de Setembro oppo-
site the Mercado Central.

TOURS AND EXCURSIONS

For **city tours** and **boat
trips** to Xefina Grande,
Inhaca Island or up the
Incomáti River, enquire at
Nkomati Safaris, tel/fax:
(1) 49-2612, probably the
most knowledgeable English-
speaking tour operators in
Maputo, or **Letoni Ferries**,
Campismo Municipal, tel/fax:
(1) 49-8139. **Ferry trips**,
jetty on Av. 10 de Novembro,
take 15 minutes across the
bay to Catembe and depart
every 30 minutes from
06:00–20:00.
On **self-guided walks** (*see*
pp. 34–39) carry only the cash
you intend to spend and
don't flaunt your camera.

USEFUL CONTACTS

Police, tel: 199.
Scuba diving tuition,
contact Inhaca Safaris,
tel: (1) 40-1642 or 40-1912.
The **Public Information
Bureau** (Bureau de Informação Publico or BIP), on
the corner of Av. Eduardo
Mondlane and Av. Francisco
Orlando Magumbwe, tel:
(1) 49-0200, fax: 49-2622,
offers helpful information,
as well as maps and books.
Dinageca, 537 Av. Josina
Machel, tel: (1) 42-3217,
fax: 42 1460. This shop
sells interesting topographic
maps of Mozambique.
**Centro Cultural Franco–
Moçambicano**, off Praça
da Independência (top of
Av. Samora Machel), tel: (1)
42-0786, fax: 42-0777. An
interesting library; offers live
traditional dancing and music
in the evenings.
Kwezi Travel, tel/fax:
(1) 40-0628 or 40-1198.
Visa service.
Clube Naval, Av. Marginal,
tel: (1) 41-2690 or 49-7674.
Yacht club.
In case of medical emergencies contact the **Clínica de
Sommerschield**, Av. Kim Il
Sung, tel: (1) 49-3924/5/6,
fax: 49-3927.

MAPUTO	J	F	M	A	M	J	J	A	S	O	N	D
AVERAGE TEMP. °F	77	75	73	73	72	68	66	68	72	77	81	77
AVERAGE TEMP. °C	25	24	23	23	22	20	19	20	22	25	27	25
RAINFALL in	6	4	4.3	2	0.7	1.2	1.5	2	1.5	1.2	3	6
RAINFALL mm	150	100	110	50	20	30	40	50	40	30	75	150

3
The Lagoon Coast

Like a string of jewels, Mozambique's **coastal lakes** stretch for 500km (311 miles) from **Ponta do Ouro** in the south as far north as **Inharrime**. Many of the lagoons and estuaries, like **Piti**, **Quissico** and **Poelela**, have been cut off from the sea by some of the world's tallest forested **sand dunes**. Others, such as the **estuaries** formed by the Maputo, Tembe and Umbulúzi rivers as well as stunning Lake (lagoa) Uembje, are open to the sea, providing protected spawning ground for the area's many fish species.

Whether you are seeking solitude on the shores of a lake, casting for game fish at the 'Cape of Currents' close to **Závora Lodge**, paddling a canoe up the **Incomáti River** estuary, exploring some of the superb **coral reefs** from **Morrungulo Lodge**, or enjoying a safari in the **Maputo Elephant Reserve**, this strip of tropical coastline promises surprises from the crest of every dune and around the next headland along each idyllic beach.

This is Da Gama's 'Terra da Boa Gente' (Land of Good People) – a reputation still deserved today, nearly 500 years after the Portuguese explorer anchored off Inharrime and was showered with gifts by the locals.

The proximity to **Maputo International Airport** (from where light aircraft may be chartered) and the wide range of accommodation on offer make the Lagoon Coast an ideal starting point for a Mozambican adventure. Base yourself at one of the charming and ideally located resorts and lodges described in this chapter and from there explore the variety and haunting beauty of the lakes and lagoons and their flora and fauna.

Don't Miss

*** Over 300 bird species: from soaring eagles to wandering albatrosses.
*** Diving: virgin coral reefs stretch for 500km (311 miles).
*** Swimming with turtles: off the Maputaland coast.
** 'World's best' shark diving: off Ponta do Ouro.
** Big game fishing: at Xai-Xai and Ponta Závora.
** Canoeing: along primeval Incomáti River estuary.
** Maputo Elephant Reserve: elephants still frequent their ancient migratory trails.

Opposite: *The pool area of the Inhaca Hotel is the best place to be on a hot day.*

NATURAL HISTORY OF INHACA

A few thousand years ago this small island was attached to the mainland. Changing sea levels and the action of wave erosion opened a channel on the southern point (**Ponta Torres**), opposite the mainland village of **Santa Maria**. The island's larger animals gradually died out due to a lack of food and Inhaca's wildlife today consists of the reefs and some 250 bird species. Walk along the sandy beach near the lighthouse and note the changing patterns of life as you move between the intertidal zones.

INHACA ISLAND (ILHA DA INHACA)

Inhaca (pronounced Inyaaka) Island lies some 24km (15 miles) from Maputo at the entrance to the bay. It is named after the chief who provided refuge for the shipwrecked early Portuguese explorers. Inhaca was probably first sighted by Europeans in 1502, when **Vasco da Gama** undertook his epic voyage around the Cape of Good Hope in search of King Solomon's legendary mines. En route to India, Da Gama was rejoined by Luis Fernandes who had been separated from the fleet during a storm at the Cape. Fernandes told of his voyage up a great river (likely to have been the Incomáti) and a bay filled with whales. This is assumed to have been Delagoa Bay which was later investigated by **Captain Lourenço Marques**.

Visitors arriving by boat are encouraged to visit the port captain, who will be able to direct them to curiosities like the market, Coconut Lodge and Lucas' Place.

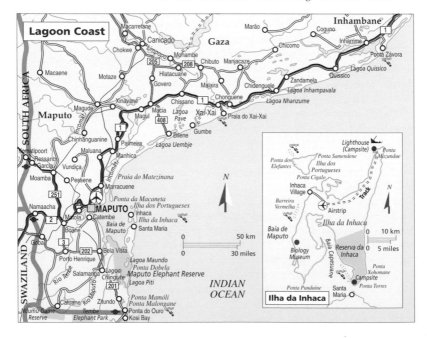

Left: *Fossils of giant marine snails such as this one have been found in Maputaland.*

MAPUTALAND

Maputaland is (loosely) the geographical area that was controlled by Chief Maputa during the early 19th century and it extends from the southern shore of Maputo Bay down into South Africa as far south as the Lake St Lucia system. **Pontas Mamóli**, **Malongane** and **do Ouro** are tourist destinations all located in the Mozambican part of Maputaland.

The **Maputaland ecosystem**, with its plains, swamps, freshwater lakes and dune forests, is unique in southern Africa. Although the Maputo reserve affords some protection to a delicate habitat, the elephant migratory route from Tembe in South Africa, along the **Fúti Channel**, is threatened by slash-and-burn agriculture, as well as by commercial forestry. The Endangered Wildlife Trust (EWT), in conjunction with a Mozambican organization, is investigating the possibility of providing some official recognition and protection for this migratory corridor.

Maputaland's Corals ★★★

Ranging in depth from 4m (13ft) to 12m (39ft), the brightly coloured soft corals (*Octocorallia*) and enormous stony corals (*Zoantharia*) in the Maputaland seas provide a refuge for hundreds of species of brilliantly marked fish and crustacea. Emperor angelfish (*Pomocanthus imperator*) with their finger-print stripes, freckled anglers (*Antennarius coccineus*) with their built-in lure, and painted surgeons (*Acanthurus leucosternon*) with their

---

INHACA IS FOR THE BIRDS

Inhaca's varied habitat attracts a great number of birds. On the island's western side, mudflats fringed by mangroves are frequented by a variety of waterbirds. A little offshore you will see hordes of gulls and terns including **lesser blackbacked gulls** as well as **Caspian** and **lesser crested terns**. A jaunt on a fishing charter usually provides sightings of **white-chinned petrels** and **shy albatrosses**. Coastal bush on the eastern hills teems with the **gorgeous bush shrike**, **grey waxbill**, **trumpeter hornbill**, **green coucal**, **gymnogene**, **Neergaard's sunbird** and **yellowspotted nicator**. If it's introduced exotics you're after, **Indian house crows**, despite efforts to eradicate them, swarm around human habitation.

Above: *Snorkelling along Maputaland's reefs is a popular tourist pastime.*

bright blue body and yellow dorsal fin, as well as the huge but friendly, brown-blotched potato bass (*Epinephelus tukula*) are just a few of the attractions of Maputaland's reefs.

Maputo Elephant Reserve ★★

Comprising 104,000ha (256,984 acres), the **Reservo dos Elefantes do Maputo** was proclaimed in 1960 in an attempt to protect the last of the herds which had been decimated by ivory traders over the centuries. The northernmost point of the reserve is the mouth of the Maputo River on Maputo Bay, while to the east is the open Indian Ocean. The peninsula which juts out towards Inhaca Island's Ponte Torres forms **Cabo de Santa Maria**, actually outside of the park.

Mangrove and reed swamps dominate the northern reaches of the Maputo reserve, while dense dune scrub and forests, interspersed with lakes Chingute, Maundo and Piti, cover the rest. The **Fúti Channel**, along which elephants migrate between Maputo and South Africa's Tembe Reserve, forms the western boundary. Maputo Reserve's 100 or so elephants are the last southern African herd still able to follow their ancient migratory routes, though this situation is threatened by poaching, slash-and-burn subsistence farming and commercial forestry.

DIVING WITH GIANT TURTLES AND EAGLE RAYS

The **leatherback turtle**, last survivor of the family *Dermochelyidae*, has a 200 million-year-old fossil history. Leatherbacks are the world's largest marine turtles, reaching 3m (10ft) in length and weighing in at an incredible 900kg (1990lb).

It is possible to swim alongside these living submarines by arranging a dive at one of the lodges on Mozambique's Maputaland coast. **Ponta dos Elefantes**, off Inhaca Island, rivals the world's best dive sites, because here **giant eagle rays** (also called manta rays) often glide past the divers.

PONTA DO OURO

The 'point of gold' which guided sailors for centuries is an unspoilt Mozambican beach that is easily accessible from South Africa. High on densely forested dunes, the lighthouse overlooks the small curved bay where vehicles are only permitted to launch boats on a small section of the sand. The motel, chalets and camp sites are tucked under shady trees, and a constant sea breeze helps to keep the malaria-carrying mosquitoes at bay. Walk south around the point, a short distance down the beach to a tatty beacon, and stand with one foot in South Africa and the other in Mozambique.

Diving at Ponta do Ouro ★★★

Within Ponta do Ouro Bay are five recognized dive sites from which to choose. Although corals are limited by the shallow depth (12–18m; 40–60ft) and the ocean surges, they do support a fantastic selection of fish life. Moray eels peer menacingly from holes, cowries display their multicoloured mantles, and the bright red tentacles of sea anemones ripple in the current.

Ponta Malongane ★★

Another of the Mozambique coast's natural geographical beacons for enthusiastic divers, Ponta Malongane now marks the position of rich coral reefs. Here a small unprotected bay nurtures a coral wonderland.

THE PEOPLE OF MAPUTALAND

Often referred to as the **Tembe-Tonga**, Maputaland's inhabitants are actually made up of diverse clans and groups. Many fled to the area during the 19th-century reign of Zulu King Shaka, who skirted Maputaland during his raids. The Tembe-Tonga still prefer to speak Zulu, however their customs are more closely related to those of the Tonga. Each homestead is built a discreet (but crucial) distance from the next, apparently to avoid quarrels with neighbours and the sometimes resulting accusations of witchcraft. Any visitor, even the chief or headman, must follow established rules of approach – standing well back until invited forward. Entrance into a hut requires permission from the owner.

Left: *A cloudburst threatens at Ponta do Ouro, border post into South Africa.*

Right: *Al fresco restaurant at Ponta Malongane in southern Mozambique.*

Kev's Ledge ★★

On the northern part of the splendid Malongane reef, at a depth of 24m (79ft), plates of hard **coral** hide nocturnal **soldiers** (*Cheimerius nufar*) and **clownfish** flirt with the poisonous tentacles of the **anemones** which provide them with protection. **Saddleback wrasse** (*Bodianus bilunulatus*) may be seen foraging for sea urchins and crabs which are then crushed by grinding plates located at the back of their mouth.

Ponta Mamóli ★

A short distance up the coast from Ponta Malongane, Ponta Mamóli is a quieter, less developed holiday spot. **Campers** will be able to make use of simple ablution facilities and water from a well. Be fully self-sufficient if you intend to visit Mamóli; telephone Ponta Malongane for the latest information. There are a couple of small stores at Ponta do Ouro village that sell basic provisions, but it would be wise to carry a good supply of food, as Ponta Malongane and Ponta Mamóli are very isolated.

Macaneta ★

The Macaneta Peninsula on the north bank of the Incomáti River is only 15km (9½ miles) from Maputo, as the crow flies. Unless you have your own boat in which to sail into the mouth of the Incomáti River, the direction of approach is via **Marracuene**, 20km (12½ miles) from

Maputo. Cross the Incomáti River by ferry (which operates from 06:00–19:00). Travel 5km (3 miles) on a sand road and you will reach a trading store where you take the right fork. Two-wheel-drive vehicles will get through although the road has a few **sand drifts** from here.

Jay's Lodge **

Secluded chalets and camp sites are hidden among the dune bush adjacent to Macaneta Beach. The fishing is excellent here and catches of kingfish and couta are a common occurrence.

The Incomáti River Camp ***

Rising near Bethal in South Africa's Mpumalanga province, and initially called the Komati River, the Incomáti crosses Swaziland before entering Mozambique at **Ressano Garcia**. On the inside of the wide meanders of the river's final bends, hidden among the dappled shade of marula and acacia trees, are tiny thatched fishing villages. Here Fernando Rodriguez (born in Mozambique and educated in South Africa) has returned to settle in his home country. Determined to contribute to the rebuilding of Mozambique, he has built a lodge for tourists, using locally produced fittings and furniture wherever possible. Fernando has been embraced by the local people, who provide fresh fish, labour and handicrafts and he offers locally produced *cerveja dois em* (2M beer), *aguardente* (fire-

---

THE GENTLE SEA TURTLES

Every year at the height of summer, **leatherback** and **loggerhead** turtles emerge from the sea at night as they have done for nearly half a million years. After dragging themselves to above the high-water mark, they dig holes, lay a few hundred eggs, pack sand on top and disguise the nest by flinging loose sand around it. Although, in theory, Mozambique's beaches are protected, in reality a lack of resources renders the legislation meaningless and local people still hunt the magnificent, docile beasts. If you have the privilege of diving with one, please share this wonderful experience with other people, to increase an awareness of the turtles' plight throughout the world.

Left: *The idyllic Incomáti River Camp, a place to relax and unwind.*

BIRD-WATCHING REQUIREMENTS

Be you 'twitcher' (seen them all) or 'ticker' (seen a few), you won't have a hope of identifying what chirps, whistles and twitters without the following:
• lightweight binoculars
• a good bird guidebook
• comfortable walking shoes, a hat and, of course, a pen. First-time birders would do well to ignore all the 'lbj's' (little brown jobs), and concentrate on the bigger, more colourful and distinctive species such as **birds of prey** and **waterbirds**. Get up with the sun or wait until late afternoon, when birds are most active.

CAMPING

Bilene has been favoured by the tent-and-caravan brigade since 1975. **Parque Flors** (flower park) is a lovely mini botanical wonderland, with waterways, wooden bridges and carpets of tropical flowers. It is also a caravan park, which along with four others, provides space for those who like to be as close to nature as a step out of the tent.

Opposite: *A quaint holiday villa, typical of the ones found at Bilene Lagoon.*
Right: *Camping under shady trees is possible on the Macaneta Peninsula.*

water) and delicious meals; feast on crab curry with cashew sauce, seafood with pasta and fresh tropical fruit salads, prepared almost entirely with ingredients available in the area. Accommodation at Incomáti is in luxurious, mosquito-proof thatch-and-wood cabins, each furnished with two beds, bedside tables and easy chairs. Most are fronted by a raised veranda, where guests can sit and contemplate the moods of the deep river as it rises and drops with the tides. The units are separated by indigenous gardens which assure seclusion and privacy and are home to brightly plumaged **sunbirds**. The entire lodge is decorated with paintings and crafts produced in Mozambique. Electricity is provided by a quietly humming generator, which is switched off in the evening. Light then falls silently from dozens of paraffin lamps.

The Incomáti River once emptied into **Maputo Bay** but was captured through erosion long ago by the Massintonto River, and now curves northwards for 100km (62 miles), before turning back to Marracuene. Sediment deposited at its mouth has formed a long sand spit which has broken up to form the **Xefina islands**. The reed beds along the river banks, and the islands that dot the lower Incomáti, provide refuge for hippos, crocodiles, dozens of species of waterbirds and massive mangrove crabs. Tidal for 30km (20 miles) of its course, the river is an important spawning ground for fish and prawns, a situation that is exploited by subsistence fisher-

men. To walk through the reed-and-thatch villages perched on the high banks of the river is to experience a way of life that has remained unchanged for centuries. The combination of the beautiful Incomáti River and the long, empty Macaneta beach (the best beach closest to Maputo) makes Macaneta well worth a few days' visit.

BILENE LAGOON (LAGOA UEMBJE)

Due to its proximity to Maputo, Bilene is the main destination for 'Maputenses' on holiday or simply taking a weekend break from the city. The town is neat, clean and offers a range of accommodation and nightlife to the visitor. If loud Angolan music, hundreds of festive people downing beer on the beach and powerboats pulling waterskiers is your idea of a holiday, spend a weekend at Bilene. Weekdays, however, are usually very quiet, a chance for you to have the place to yourself.

To get to this pretty resort village with its 20km-long (12½-mile) and 5km-wide (3-mile) lagoon, take the EN1 for 160km (100 miles) north to **Macia**. Here turn right onto a good paved road, and continue for 30km (20 miles) to a traffic circle just after which you'll see **Hotel Bilene**. Although open for business, hotel staff may have trouble finding you a room in a state fit for occupation. Carry on downhill past the left of the hotel, and one of the freshwater lakes which make up the complex Bilene water system, can be seen at the bottom of the valley to the left.

IS BILENE LAGOON OPEN TO THE SEA?

Bilene Lagoon or, more accurately, **Lagoa Uembje**, is a favourite spot for deep-sea fishermen. The **Mozambique Current**, which pushes powerfully through Mozambique Channel, is at its closest to the coast here. **Longshore drift** carries sand from the north and deposits it in the lagoon mouth, often causing blockage, but efforts to open the lagoon using earth-moving equipment have proved ineffective. By the end of the rainy season (November–April), Bilene Lagoon usually fills to a point where it flows over the sandbar into the sea, thus flushing out the mouth. Ski-boaters, confined before to the sterile inland lake, can only then roar out to the fishing grounds in the open sea.

Above: *A carpenter in Xai-Xai produces another lovely piece of furniture.*
Opposite: *Time for quiet reflection at the beautiful Lagoa Piti.*

XAI-XAI

Perched on the northern bank of the **Limpopo River**, 224km (135 miles) north of Maputo, is the medium-sized town of Xai-Xai, the capital of Gaza province. Xai-Xai, with a population of over 100,000, has wide avenues lined with flamboyant trees, and offers ice (*gelo*), service stations, supermarkets, open-air markets, restaurants, international telephones, banks and a hospital. Clean toilets (a luxury anywhere in Mozambique) can be found at the first BP service station on your left, after crossing the toll bridge (a small fee is levied) over the Limpopo River.

Praia do Xai-Xai *

On the northern outskirts of Xai-Xai town, turn down to **Xai-Xai beach**, 10km (6 miles) away. A favourite fishing spot of South African anglers, Xai-Xai tends to be busy during the South African school holidays (June–July and December–January). The beaches here are long and clean, however due to its exposed position Xai-Xai has developed a reputation for being somewhat windswept.

Walking 7km (4½ miles) north from the developed area, you will encounter **Praia do Chonguene** with the abandoned Hotel Chonguene (which is slowly sliding into the sea). On the nearby beach are the remnants of a rusty shipwreck almost completely covered by sand. A large tidal pool known as **Wenela** (after a house owned by the recruitment agency of the same name), which overlooks the pool, lies 5km (3 miles) south of Xai-Xai beach. A large blowhole in the reef is exposed at low tide, but do beware of swimming near it due to the treacherous currents. To members of the African Pentecostal Church, Wenela is 'Jordan', a holy place where colourful baptism ceremonies are held.

THE LAKES

Most motorists just bypass **Quissico**, a 'one-street town' with a colourful market; but by bothering to go just 800m (½ mile) off the main road to Quissico's administration building at the end of a tree-lined avenue, you will reach one of the best viewsites in Mozambique. Azure-blue **Lake Quissico** (200m; 660ft) below, with its palm-fringed white beaches, stretches to the horizon from left to right. The darker shade of blue straight out in front, across high forested dunes, is the Indian Ocean.

Lagoa Inhampavala *

Not visible from the EN1, this isolated stretch of inland water is surrounded by thickly wooded dunes. The beach lies only a short walk across. Herons, cormorants, flamingos and kingfishers inhabit the reed-fringed shores. Although the water is pleasant for swimming, its high salt content makes it unpalatable for drinking. Sweet water can be collected from a spring close to where the road crosses the southern end of the lake.

Ponta Závora *

During the South African and Zimbabwean school holiday periods, Závora is packed with sport fishermen and their families, consequently the facilities available fit the needs of this group. The reefs off Závora are reputed to offer some of Mozambique's best spear-fishing opportunities. Camping is possible in a large area on the landward side of the dunes, with chalets on the seaward end. As there is a fair amount of swampland around, mosquitoes can be a pest when the air is still. A small, well-stocked general store is always open. Fishing and diving charters may be organized by special arrangement, and an airstrip is being built.

MOZAMBIQUE'S LAKE DISTRICT

Stretching from **Chidenguele** on the EN1, 260km (161 miles) north of Maputo to **Ponta São Sebastião** further up the coast, a dozen freshwater lakes grace the coastline. From Inhazume and Inhampavala to Muangani and Manhali, these lakes show that Mozambique's coastline has periodically receded and advanced during a recent geological period. Tectonic forces as well as coastal erosion have combined to remove sand from some places, depositing it elsewhere, forming dunes, spits and sand islands.

The Lagoon Coast at a Glance

BEST TIMES TO VISIT

From **May** to **October** is the **coolest** and **driest** period, when the risk of malaria is lowest. Average temperatures may remain above 20°C (68°F) but **cold snaps** do occur. **December** and **January** may be the **warmest** period but the concurrent **high rainfall** (250mm; 10in) per month, has a cooling effect.

GETTING THERE

The easiest and most convenient access to **Ponta do Ouro, Ponta Malongane** and **Ponta Mamóli**, though suitable for 4WD vehicles only, is from South Africa. However, many resorts are able to collect their visitors from the border. Some 20km (12½ miles) before Kosi Bay (KwaZulu-Natal) you reach Kwa Ngwanase (Manguzi) village. At the fork after the Kwiksave supermarket, turn left and continue for 25km (15½ miles) on an increasingly sandy track, to the Farazella (Ponta do Ouro) control post. From here it's another 12km (7½ miles) through **deep dune sand** to Ponta do Ouro. Pontas Mamóli and Malongane are 10km (6 miles) further up the coast.

To reach **Bela Vista** from Maputo, ferry your car to Catembe, and follow 42km (26 miles) of potholed road. After Bela Vista, turn left and cross the Maputo River

to enter the renowned **Maputo Elephant Reserve**. Please note that roads in the park are suitable for 4WD drive vehicles only, and you must have a permit, issued in Maputo, tel:(1) 43-1789.

To reach **Lagoa Quissico** and the beach, if you're coming from the south, shortly after passing **Quissico** town, turn right and follow the 11km (7-mile) dirt road (for 4WD only) which runs between the two largest lakes.

To reach **Závora Lodge** drive to the signposted turn off 12km (7 miles) from Inharrime, from where it is another 25km (15½ miles) to Praia de Závora.

Inhaca Island is accessible by speedboat, ferry and by air. **Letoni Ferries** (see p. 43) will transfer you in swift twin-hulled boats, at reasonable rates. **Incomáti River Lodge** meets its guests either at Maputo International Airport or at the Incomáti ferry terminal on the outskirts of Marracuene 30km (20 miles) north of Maputo. Public transport in this region is fairly regular and reliable.

GETTING AROUND

The best buses are operated by **Transportes Oliveiras** (see p. 42). Buses to Beira leave from the terminus (Praça 16 de Junho, Maputo) every morning at 06:30.
N**o buses** or regular *chapas*

are available to **Ponta do Ouro**. In **Catembe** ask for **supply trucks** doing the run south. The drivers may give you a ride for a small fee, but since this is not a scheduled service be prepared to wait for a few days.

Air charter companies available are Sabin Air, tel: (1) 46-5108, fax: 46-5011, and STA Air Charters, tel: (1) 49-1765.

The **EN1** (Estrada Nacional), which is in good condition as far north as the Rio Save, is the main access route to places north of Maputo like Macaneta, Bilene, Xai-Xai and the lakes.

WHERE TO STAY

Inhaca Island
MID-RANGE
Hotel Inhaca, tel: (1) 42-9277, fax: 42-0524. Bungalow-style rooms; swimming pool. Fishing and diving trips arranged.

BUDGET
Coconut Lodge, Inhaca Island, an hour's walk from the hotel. No telephone. Chalets and camping; running water.

Ponta do Ouro
MID-RANGE
Complexo Turístico Ponta do Ouro, tel: (2711) 425-2866, Benoni, South Africa. Camping sites and fully serviced cottages.

Motel do Mar, Ponto do Ouro, tel: (2712) 43-2846 Pretoria, South Africa. Basic but clean.

The Lagoon Coast at a Glance

Ponta Malongane
MID-RANGE
Fully equipped, serviced chalets and rondavels, tel: (2712) 348-4262, Pretoria, South Africa. Comfortable accommodation; scuba diving and deep-sea fishing.

Macaneta
MID-RANGE
Jay's Chalets and Camping Site, Praia de Matezinana, tel: (1) 49-3533. Landscaped grounds; shady camping sites and luxury 4-bed chalets.

Marracuene
LUXURY
Incomáti River Camp, Marracuene, tel: (1) 49-2612, fax: (1) 49-8139, or Pretoria, South Africa, tel: (2712) 343-2957. A piece of paradise! Bookings are essential.

Bilene
BUDGET
The Palm Tree, on the beach road north, Bilene, tel: (22) 2-2939. There is a restaurant, camping sites and 4-bed chalets.

Xai-Xai
BUDGET
Xai-Xai Beach Caravan Park, tel: (022) 2-2942. Camping and bungalows as well as a rustic beach bar.

Ponta Závora
BUDGET
Závora Lodge, contact Gone Fishin' in Johannesburg, South Africa, tel: (2711) 609-7806. 8-sleeper cottages, 6-sleeper houses. Fishing and diving charters are possible by special arrangement; booking is essential for non campers.

WHERE TO EAT
Budget travellers should head for the markets, because many of the resorts are self-catering.

Inhaca Island
Lucas', Inhaca village near the hotel. Traditional fare.

Ponta Malongane
The beach restaurant offers tasty and affordable meals.

Macaneta
Restaurante Macaneta, Macaneta Point, tel: (1) 3-4096. Pub; good seafood; somewhat pricey.

Bilene
Pavilho Tamar, Bilene, tel: (22) 2-2946. Open from 07:00; overlooks the lagoon. Patron Luis Tavares is an outstanding chef.

TOURS AND EXCURSIONS
Maputo Elephant Reserve, tel: (1) 49-2612, fax: 49-8139. Unless you are booked into the **Msala Bush Camp**, access is restricted. 'Rubber ducks' (dinghies) can be hired at **The Palm Tree** on Bilene Lagoon and one is available to the guests of the **Incomáti River Lodge**, who also have canoes at their disposal.
Nkomati Safaris (see p. 43) arrange custom tours to the entire Lagoon Coast area.
Scuba divers should get in touch with **BLU** (Ponta do Ouro), tel/fax: (2711) 465-9624, Johannesburg, South Africa; alternatively get in touch with **Intercontinental Explorers** (at Ponta Malongane) who operate from Pretoria, South Africa, tel: (2712) 348-4262. Full scuba gear can be hired, diving courses for first-timers are offered and dive boats are available.
Exciting fishing safaris to a number of coastal fishing spots, as well as Cahora Bassa may be arranged through **Fish Africa**, tel: (2711) 888-3168, Johannesburg, South Africa.

USEFUL CONTACTS
Fishermen should contact **Luis Tavares**, Bilene, tel: (22) 2-2946, who is able to supply invaluable information regarding the best spots, and also organizes tours.
In the event of a medical emergency contact one of the following:
Red Cross Ambulance, Maputo, tel: (1) 42-9554.
Police Ambulance, Maputo, tel: (1) 42-2001 or 42-5001. Useful tourist information can be supplied by **Mozambique Holiday Services**, Maputo, tel: (1) 49-3025.

4
Inhambane and Surrounds

Inhambane province and its capital of the same name lie outside the destructive path of the tropical cyclones that sometimes wreak havoc along southern Africa's east coast. The isolation of this region has ensured its virtual escape from unsavoury modern influences – as a result, much cultural and historical heritage has been retained.

The **road** to the clean port town of **Inhambane**, a mere day's journey by bus or car from Maputo in the south, is tarred and in good condition, having been spared the destruction of the past civil upheaval. Although, at present, no scheduled flights serve the town, the nearby **airport** is capable of handling **large jets** and is used by various air charter companies. Travellers with an **adventurous spirit** and no particular deadlines ahead, may want to investigate the (irregular) **dhow** traffic between Beira, Vilankulo and Inhambane. Although this option is not the safest or most comfortable, it is definitely the most romantic. The jetties at **Maxixe** and Inhambane are the southernmost anchorage for Arab dhows, known colloquially as *ingalāoa* or *barcos as velas*, graceful ancient craft that are still being built in the tiny coastal villages lining the bay.

Within a 30km (18-mile) radius of Inhambane town lie half a dozen destinations well worth a visit. From legendary **Linga Linga Peninsula**, at the entrance to **Baia de Inhambane** (where **dugongs** are often spotted), and the serene sands of **Ponta da Barra** to the prolific marine life of Pandane's beautiful **Lighthouse Reef**, visitors can expect a cultural, natural and visual feast.

DON'T MISS

*** Linga Linga: diving with the gentle dugongs is an unforgettable experience.
*** Dhow race: a hundred dhows race across Inhambane Bay in November.
** Fishing: marlin and sailfish can be caught from the beaches at Pomene.
** Snorkelling: off Pandane lies a natural aquarium.
** Dhow taxi: a unique mode of transport from Maxixe to Inhambane.
* Roadside stalls: refreshing oranges and *lanhos* (young coconuts) for sale in summer.

Opposite: *Dhows lie at anchor in Inhambane Bay.*

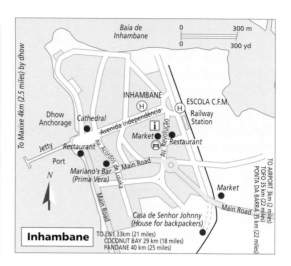

INHAMBANE BAY

Travelling on the EN1, you will know you are approaching the provincial capital Inhambane when coconut palms begin to dominate the landscape. To reach the town, turn off at Lindela and then continue for 33km (20 miles).

During the first part of the 15th century, **Portuguese explorers** established a permanent trading post here, making Inhambane one of the oldest European settlements in southern Africa. Lying on the eastern shore of the large sheltered **Bay of Inhambane**, the sleepy and neat town has about 50,000 inhabitants. There is an **airport** suitable for large aircraft and the town also has **port facilities** capable of accommodating ships with a displacement of up to 10,000 tonnes.

Hundreds of graceful dhows on the usually tranquil water are one of Inhambane's most obvious features. The seamanship and boat-building skills of Inhambane's *marinheiros* (sailors) and *pescadores* (fishermen) are legendary, and the little town probably has the largest working fleet of dhows (around 200) on the entire East African coastline. Likely reasons for this statistic may be found in Inhambane's calm location outside the cyclone belt, as well as in the recent past when roads were often impassable.

Until the mid-1960s, Inhambane was a very crowded little harbour. The cranes on the jetty were kept busy loading tons of copra, peanuts, oil seed, cotton, rice, sugar and cashew nuts. Those were the days when over a million migrant mine-workers commuted regularly between Mozambique and South Africa's gold-rich Witwatersrand (now Gauteng). A packet boat transported these men to the then Lourenço Marques from where they were taken to the mines by train. Although most of the area's produce is now transported to Maputo harbour by road, coasters still call at Inhambane on an irregular basis to offload consumer goods and load copra and cashews.

The Inhambane district is notorious for the brewing of powerful **illicit liquor** from cashews, pineapples, mangoes and oranges; in short, any fruit available. Known as *enhica*, the highly intoxicating effect of this

COCONUT REPUBLIC

The coconut palm (*Cocos nucifera*), of which there are nearly two million in the Inhambane area, produces about 22.5kg (50 lb) of coconuts each year. Individual trees are owned by families who send their youngest sons to collect palm sap for the production of a potent wine called *sura*. Inhambane's soil and climate are ideal for the palms – which only thrive in frost-free areas – so much so that trees take about five years to bear fruit (as opposed to seven in other areas), produce for about 40 years and live for up to 80. It appears that a rule of thumb is: 'the nearer the sea, the better the crop'

Left: *Two Inhambane boys on a wide street look suspiciously into the camera.*

A WORKING 'MUSEUM'

From Inhambane jetty walk down Av. Independência, right into Av. Acordos de Lusaka and a few blocks to the **Prima Vera Restaurant** (Mariano's Bar) – next door is a fascinating working 'museum'. Politely ask permission to walk around this little **printing shop** which, far from being a formal museum, still produces such stationery items as invitations and invoice books. Every letter and character is first fixed on brass blocks and then placed by hand on manual presses. Most 60-year-old printing machines are regarded as antiques and displayed behind glass, but not in Mozambique. For decades all development stood still and so the country remains caught in a time warp.

concoction on the locals is particularly noticeable during cashew season (from November to March).

When it was still a province of Portugal, **Antonio Enes**, a past governor general of Mozambique, referred to this moonshine as the 'root of vice and ruin'. One of his reports reads: 'In the season of this accursed fruit, when the atmosphere is poisoned by the resinous odours of the fat jugs displayed in the markets, and in the taverns, Native (sic) labourers leave their hoes, carriers abandon their loads, servants flee their masters, soldiers and sailors desert. Vagrancy and saturnalia continue so long as the supplies of drink last.'

A hotel, shops, markets, bus terminus and immigration office (visa extensions here) are all to be found in pleasant Inhambane. The dhows, fragrant spice and colourful cloth **markets**, **mosques** and little Indian-owned stores lend an oriental atmosphere to the streets. Inhambane Bay was the southernmost point down the Mozambique Channel to which **Arab** and **Persian traders** travelled. From about the 10th century until the mid-20th century, slaves, hardwoods, gold and other metals collected from the East African interior were exchanged for cloth, salt and beads.

Left: *The Cathedral of Our Lady of the Conception, in Inhambane, is 200 years old.*
Opposite: *A variety of goods is available from the market at Inhambane.*

Sightseeing in Inhambane ***

Whether arriving at Inhambane by dhow or car, people will inevitably end up at the port, where the magnificent **new cathedral** (open on Sundays) and the long L-shaped **jetty** are obvious landmarks. Alongside the modern cathedral, the 200-year-old **Cathedral of Our Lady of the Conception** is worth entering. Climb up into the bell tower for sublime views of the bay and town. Avenida Independência stretches directly from the jetty. On this wide, tree-lined thoroughfare you will come across the **Hotel Inhambane** which, until renovated, should be used in emergencies only. **Garagem São Cristovão** offers petrol (*gasolina*), diesel (*gasóleo*), paraffin (*petróleo*) and engine oil (*óleo de lubrificar*). This service station has the distinction of being one of the few places around where clean toilets and air to pump up your vehicle's tyres are also available. You will pass major banks and the colonial-style municipal offices, before reaching the large traffic circle at the end of the avenue.

Apart from Avenida Independência, three other avenues lead off from this circle. Straight ahead is the **railway station** and **shunting yard** where old train engines stand and sadly rust away. Walk a little way up the quaint road called **Avenida Revolução** and you will find **Restaurante Tic Tic**, popular among the locals. The interesting municipal market, Mercado Municipal, close by is definitely worth exploring.

BASKET WEAVERS

Walk down Av. Revolução and a little past the **Restaurante Tic Tic**, and you'll reach the **Mercado Municipal**, a market that offers a bewildering selection of baskets, mats, hats and other useful household items. Prices are low by Western standards, but don't be tempted to pay more, as this only pushes prices out of reach of the populace.
A **reed basket** is probably one of the most worthwhile purchases you can make as plastic bags are scarce, especially in northern Mozambique. Women cut reeds from the fringes of mangrove swamps and weave them while they are still green and pliable. Stroll into any of Inhambane's *bairros*, and you'll find the weavers sitting in front of their houses, hard at work.

Another picturesque street well worth exploring, especially if your stomach is beginning to rumble, is the **Avenida Acordos de Lusaka**. From the Inhambane jetty walk down the right-hand side of Av. Independência. One block down turn right into the **Acordos de Lusaka** (don't expect to see any signpost) and another two blocks along this road, on your right, you will find the **Restaurante Prima Vera** (Mariano's Bar) where the locals congregate regularly.

Mariano, the owner, has weathered 50 years of change in Inhambane. He is considered an important (and helpful) man in the community and therefore all visitors are expected to 'check in' with him upon arrival. You are advised to follow this custom.

Dhow Taxis ***

A short, cheap ride by **dhow**, from Inhambane's jetty across the bay to the town of **Maxixe**, is a tempting alternative to the dusty, 62km (38-mile) trip around the bay by road. Backpackers, of course, will opt for the wind-powered option, but if your party has arrived by car you may as well draw straws to see which one of you will have to do the driving around.

You may have to wait a while until there are enough passengers to warrant the dhow's departure, so why not sample a few refreshments at the **Snack-Bar Ti Jamu**, at the beginning of the walkway, which is an ideal spot for

---

DHOW RACE

Cowes Week is just a cruise around the dam compared to this spectacle of epic proportions. In **November** each year the provincial governor sponsors a dhow race on **Inhambane Bay**. The competitors take this event very seriously as the prize money amounts to as much as a year's earnings. Plan to be in the area during the **Corrida de Barcos a Vela** and you could witness, or even take part in, this unique challenge (dhows are for hire).

admiring the dhows on the bay, especially at sunset. Adhering to a quaint tradition that dates back hundreds of years, the dhow crew will insist on carrying you to and from their boat, a unique and old-fashioned service that is offered with genuine enthusiasm.

Dhows are as synonymous with Inhambane as yellow cabs are with New York City. Walk into any of the villages along the shores of Inhambane Bay that are accessible from the main road and you will come across skilled *carpinteiros* (carpenters) building new vessels using traditional tools and techniques that have been handed down for generations.

The origin of the name *dhow* remains unclear, but what is known is that these craft originated in the seas off Arabia. The ocean-going variety, which displaced up to as much as 200 tonnes, was used for the slave trade until 1860. Today, dhows that big are very scarce, but the 'modern' ones still display the characteristic lateen (triangular) sail, a single, short wooden mast and a very long yard (crosswise spar) which is rigged at an angle of 45° when the vessel is underway.

SHE-OAKS

The she-oaks or casuarinas (*Casuarinaceae*) are made up of a group of 45 highly distinctive semi-evergreen trees and shrubs native to northeast Australia, Southeast Asia, New Caledonia, Fiji and the Mascarene Islands. Casuarinas are tall trees, with slender but wiry shoots which 'weep' (give off a light sap that soils tents, cars and anything else left underneath them). Common along the entire length of the coast, the Mozambican casuarina (*Casuarina equisetifolia*), also known as the horsetail tree, South Sea ironwood and she-oak, grows well in brackish soils, and was planted to stabilize the sand dunes and to form a windbreak. The name 'she-oak' derives from the resemblance of the tree's long thin pine needles to women's hair.

Opposite: *Dhow taxis line up for trade at Maxixe.*
Left: *A dhow offloads its passengers at the Maxixe ferry jetty.*

EXECUTION ROCK

Around the shoreline along Tofo beach is a grassy mound on a small peninsula. Short limestone cliffs drop into the ocean where waves shoulder the rock relentlessly. This is **Ponta Verde** and here stand the remnants of a socialist sculpture glorifying the victories of Frelimo. Just beyond this structure is a deep, narrow gulley, where bones of the victims of 'kangaroo' courts (summary trials held without proper proceedings or witnesses) could be found. If you are willing to risk climbing down this crevice, you could still find the odd femur or skull. But if you slip, your skeleton might become a tourist attraction too!

TOFO VILLAGE AND BARRA BEACH

Driving east from Inhambane, you will skirt mangroves and coconut plantations on the way to Tofo. When the wind blows through this once busy fishing resort, it seems as though the voices of the ghosts of raucous big-game fishermen echo softly down the deserted streets. And yet Tofo is changing, buildings are being renovated, the hotel is open for business and the **Clube Ferroviáro** (Railway Club) now provides comfortable rooms.

Visitors should bring along a supply of food as Tofo's only restaurant and the hotel may produce fine meals on occasion, but they are often closed for no apparent reason. Tofo fronts onto a small bay fringed by a pristine, wide and white beach which stretches north as far as **Ponta da Barra** (sandbar point), and to the south, a short distance around a rocky headland, is a coral-lined bay called **Tofinho**.

BARRA PENINSULA AND CAPE INHAMBANE

When viewed from the air or on a large-scale map, Inhambane Bay resembles a river delta in many respects. However, the geomorphological processes that have produced the channels, sandbanks, island and spits that make up the Barra peninsula and Cape Inhambane have, in fact, worked in an opposite way to

those producing deltas (where sand, carried down to the sea by rivers, is deposited and subsequently splits into channels). At Inhambane Bay, the sand carried by the northward-moving longshore counter-currents is constantly being deposited at the mouth of Inhambane Bay. Sandbars form, in time becoming spits and small bare islands, ideal places for mangrove trees to colonize and thus stabilize. In this region the process is at an advanced stage as evidenced by the extensive mangrove swamps encountered between Inhambane town and Cape Inhambane.

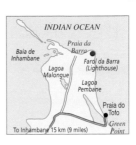

As the seabed dips steeply away from the shore, causing large waves and therefore strong currents which enter the bay, Tofo can be a somewhat treach-erous swimming beach for the unwary. Snorkellers and scuba divers should always leave one of their party on the beach to summon help in an emergency, and limit their outings to periods when the tide is coming in. Bathers are warned to swim and surf only directly in front of the hotel as strong **rip currents** prevail on the left (when facing the sea). Surfing can be excellent if the tide is right at **Tofinho**, or 'little Tofo', around the headland to the right, before you reach the recently vandalized monument. It is also a wise precaution not to tempt the villagers by leaving any unattended belongings on the shore.

Opposite: *The hotel at Tofo is located right on the beautiful, unspoilt beach.*
Left: *Tofo Beach – paradise for sunbathers, swimmers and surfers.*

Right: *Pandane Beach has some of the best snorkelling sites in Mozambique.*
Opposite: *The lovely stretch of coastline between Coconut Bay and Pandane.*

Camping at Tofo and Tofinho *

Independent travellers often pitch their tents somewhere on the beach and then fend for themselves regarding food, water and ablutions. There is a well, so bring along your own 20-litre (5-gallon) container. You'll be able to buy fish on the beach, and fruit and vegetables are sold at the cruzamento (crossroads) 5km (3 miles) away.

Note that the twin irritations of **mosquitoes** and petty thieving could ruin your stay, so remember to bring mosquito nets and repellent, and employ a *guarda* (guard). Always lock everything out of sight, in a vehicle if possible, and don't flaunt any valuable items.

Ponta da Barra **

The route to Ponta da Barra from Inhambane is similar to that to Tofo, but when you get to the cruzamento (look for Bar Babalaza), carry on straight onto a road which becomes increasingly sandy. Although accessible for skilful drivers in a Kombi or pickup truck with the tyre pressure reduced to 100kpi (1 bar), until the planned improvements are made, getting to Barra is possible by 4WD only.

Of course you can catch a *chapa* to the cruzamento, and then walk the last 7km (4½ miles) to the beach. Wayne and Lillee of **Barra Lodge** will welcome you to their section of one of the most secluded and beautiful beaches in Mozambique.

MAURICE'S TALE

Maurice, the **Ponta da Barra lighthouse keeper**, is full of tales of times gone by. He recalls the days when he was paid by Portugal and his lamps burned with paraffin; today the beam is solar-powered, and he is not sure who pays him. Like Maurice, many folk are not here simply for the fishing and diving, and if you are a visitor of the more curious persuasion, draw closer to the point: watch the sunrise over the water where two opposing currents meet; jog down to Tofo and back; walk along the beach to the mouth of the mangrove estuary and at low tide, walk into the swamp and marvel at this delicate, complex ecosystem.

COCONUT BAY (BAIA DOS COCOS) AND PANDANE

Cocos is a destination especially for the 'life-is-too-short-to-play-golf' fraternity. Tainted water can be drawn from a well, but the manager sells bottled water, beer and cold drinks, so you need not risk the 'runs'. Do chew through a few coconuts while here (in deference to the insightful person who named the place, you understand). You have the opportunity to buy ice at the fish factory (Pescom) opposite the turnoff, from the Inhambane–EN1 road, down a sandy track to the somewhat ramshackle Coconut Bay camp site.

Pandane (Praia de Jangamo) **

Pandane is an exciting and wonderful **snorkelling paradise**. A superb inland reef, which is only a few metres deep at high tide, is protected from destruction by the powerful currents, waves and surges by a sand bar. Visibility under the surface is usually at least 20m (65ft) and can be as much as 40m (130ft), making Pandane beach one of the very best snorkelling spots on the East African coast.

SEA OF ZANJ

The sea of Bahr-el-Zanj lies between the Tropic of Capricorn and the Equator, from the east coast of Africa to beyond the Mascarene Islands (Mauritius, Réunion and Rodrigues). South African writer, T V Bulpin, wrote in 1957: 'In the Arabian Nights there was such a sea. Sinbad knew it well, although in after years its name was quite forgotten. It was a fabulous sea of countless islands, strange and magic. It was a sea which nursed a lost world inhabited by nightmare creatures wandering through a whole greenhouse of fantastic plants. It was a sea of legends where dwelt the Roc, that monstrous bird which, it was whispered, could carry an entire elephant in its talons. It was a mysterious wilderness of waters, a backblock of the Indian Ocean where the great rollers came sweeping in towards the shores of Mother Africa. It was the sea known to the Arabs by the ancient, long forgotten, but most honoured name of Bahr-el-Zanj.'

MAXIXE AND SURROUNDS

About 460km (285 miles) from Maputo, Maxixe (pronounced 'Masheesh') is the only section of the EN1 which touches onto the long Mozambique coastline. Maxixe is therefore an obvious place for travellers, from both the north and south, to kick off their travelling boots and get some sand between their toes. Maxixe's jetty, just 50m (165ft) across the road from the Mobil service station, is one of the world's last major dhow staging posts. The EN1 passes between the town and the bay, so apart from the **Campismo da Maxixe** (camp site) all other facilities are on your left, if travelling north, and on your right, if travelling south. Alongside the EN1 there are two service stations (Mobil and 2M Petromoc). You will be able to find limited spares and repair facilities at Mobil.

Ponta Linga Linga **

Linga Linga is not to be missed if you have a (slightly) adventurous spirit and a desire to experience non-commercialized, uncomplicated Mozambique. Dhows do leave for Linga Linga from the Inhambane jetty, but the easiest way to get there is from Maxixe. Get

Right: *Passengers line up at the ferry jetty of Maxixe.*

down to the jetty, put out word that you're headed for Linga Linga, and soon a dhow will be at your disposal. For the same price per day as half a dozen beers, this *ingalāoa* or *barco a vela* will be at your disposal for as long as you wish. If the wind is right, the trip will take three to four hours, but if it fails, prepare yourself for an uncomfortable wait. The sun is the worst enemy of becalmed sailors, so take a *capulana* (sarong) to rig up for shade

Linga Linga is the focus of some schemes to develop it into an ecotourist destination, but a lack of potable water and its remote location are hampering efforts. Be fully self-sufficient if you are heading here, and include enough drinking water (10 litres, or 20 pints, per person per day is recommended). An accommodating architect, Mike, the manager, may or may not be at Linga Linga to welcome you, but his staff will fill his shoes admirably.

Massinga *

With its carpentry shops and colourful market, Massinga is worthy of a closer look on your way to somewhere else. The true significance of Massinga will

Above: *Rustic chalets at Campismo de Maxixe invite you to stay.*

CREATURES OF THE CORALS

Coral reefs provide a habitat for a large variety of organisms which rely on the coral for food and shelter. Decapod crustaceans such as **shrimps** and **crabs**, as well as fish like the **parrotfish** (*Scaridae*) depend on corals for shelter. **Sponges** inhabiting coral cavities as a protection from predators remove small chips of calcium carbonate from their hosts, thereby causing bio-erosion. Other organisms that inhabit the reefs are **crown-of-thorn starfish**, **sea urchins**, **jellyfish**, **clams**, **oysters**, **turtles** and colourful **sea anemones**.

Right: *Another hard day at Morrungulo Lodge!*
Opposite: *Waves roll into beautiful Nelson's Bay.*

only be revealed to those unfortunate enough to damage an essential part of their car in the area. Behind one of the two filling stations in Massinga, there is an excellent little workshop, where a **mechanic** (*mecânico*) does an excellent job of welding up broken bits of suspension or chassis.

Nelson's Bay (Morrungulo) ★★★

This divine little **coconut grove** with its beach-fringed bay is primarily a sport fishing and diving location. The first stunning views of the camping area are of lush green grass under gently swaying coconut palms – and a few steps away unspoilt, glistening white sands stretch in an arc from horizon to horizon. This is delightful Nelson's Bay, named after the Zimbabwean family who owned the resort before 1975, and who, by buying the coconut palms, managed to hold onto it through the dark years when the tourists stayed away. The Nelsons still own **Morrungulo Lodge**, and it is once more filled with Zimbabwean and South African families during the school holidays.

Pomene *

Pomene and Ponta da Barra Falsa are on the point of a large peninsula reached via an extremely sandy, almost impassable track. The once-famous hotel now lies in ruins, but fishermen do still occasionally set up their own camps here.

In the past, owners of 4WD 'bakkies' (pickups) made use of the road to Morrungulo Lodge to reach the beach, before heading north along the beach to Pomene. Quite apart from the fact that it is illegal to drive on the beaches without a permit, the management at Morrungulo will turn you around if you are not staying on their premises.

There are plans afoot to rehabilitate the Pomene complex and surrounds, but until then this usually deserted spot has no facilities at all. You will have to wait for a while before seeing for yourself whether those tales of the good old days, when sailfish and marlin were caught from the beach, still hold or not.

SYLVIA SHOAL

In his book *Beneath Southern Seas*, Tim Condon writes of Sylvia Shoal (2km; 1¼ miles from Morrungulo): 'They abound in everything the sea has to offer, and every moment is like a chapter out of a Jules Verne novel. Indeed, I sincerely believe that, until a diver has dived on Sylvia Shoal, he (sic) has never dived at all.' If the idea of diving with giant manta rays, docile whale sharks and big leatherback turtles appeals to you then Sylvia Shoal, by all reports, is a good bet.

Inhambane and Surrounds at a Glance

BEST TIMES TO VISIT

April to **September**, though still very warm, is the **cooler** and **drier** period. The town of Inhambane lies on the edge of the cyclone belt, and **strong winds** (up to 110kph; 68mph), as well as torrential downpours, can occur from January to March. **Hottest** and most **humid** is **November** to **February**, when the risk of **malaria** is highest too.

GETTING THERE

Although Inhambane has an excellent airport, it is not served by LAM flights. **Air charter** can be arranged from Maputo (see p. 42). Transportes Oliveiras **buses** travel to Inhambane regularly from towns north and south along the EN1, but since this town presents a 33km (20 mile) deviation from the main road some buses stop only at Maxixe, from where dhows cross Inhambane Bay from dawn till dusk.

GETTING AROUND

The tarmac road to **Tofo** is in good condition. In Inhambane turn right at the end of Av. da Independência, opposite the station, and follow the road parallel to the railway line. At the traffic circle turn left, cross the railway and after about 19km (12 miles) you will reach a crossroads. Carry on straight to **Ponta da Barra**; turn right for Tofo.

6.5km (4 miles) before you reach Inhambane, turn right at a fish factory that also sells ice, and cross the railway line onto a sand track (4WD) – **Coconut Bay** is about 22km (13 miles) away and **Pandane Beach** lies 12km (7½ miles) further south.

The turnoff to **Nelson's Bay** (Morrungulo) is 6km (4 miles) from Massinga, toward the sea. 13km (8 miles) from the EN1 along a passable track you will come to a **cycad garden** and Morrungulo's reception building. Fly-in guests land at Massinga's 1000m (3281ft) airstrip – transfer to the Dive Centre takes about 30 minutes.

WHERE TO STAY

Inhambane
BUDGET
Hotel Inhambane, 57 Av. Independência, tel: (23) 2855. Threadbare, self-contained rooms; reasonable rates.

Tofo and Ponta da Barra
MID-RANGE
Barra Lodge Beach Resort, Ponta da Barra. To book call Phokwane, South Africa, tel: (2713) 719-9772. Camping, self-catering cottages, bunkhouse, bar and restaurant. For **Scuba diving** trips call Johannesburg, tel: (2711) 314-3239.

BUDGET
Complexo Turístico do Tofo Mar (Tofo Hotel).

To book call Maputo, tel: (1) 42-7352 after hours, alternatively write to PO Box 66, Inhambane. Fairly threadbare rooms; intermittently running water; prices tend to be somewhat negotiable.

Maxixe
BUDGET
Campismo da Maxixe, PO Box 149, Maxixe, Provincia de Inhambane, tel: (23) 2351, speak to Erwin Jakes. An oasis of security, shade and service with beach houses and 2-bed cottages, camping and 'Overland Truck' sites (with 220 V power), as well as a backpacker 'tent town' (bring your own tent). Ablutions and security are some of the best in Mozambique. All the water here is drinkable borehole water. Foreign visitors are expected to pay in SARand or US$, no credit cards accepted. Pets not allowed. Secure parking for folk heading up to **Linga Linga** for a couple of days.

Pandane
BUDGET
Lighthouse Reef, contact Lee Booysen, tel: (2713) 719-9772, South Africa. Furnished chalets, shady camp sites, and an idyllic beach.

Nelson's Bay
LUXURY
Morrungulo Dive Centre, to book call Pretoria, South

Inhambane and Surrounds at a Glance

Africa, tel: (2712) 998-9989.Camping sites and luxury chalets; full board.

MID-RANGE
Morrungulo Resort Area, tel: (2634) 30-3504, fax: 30-3504, Harare, Zimbabwe and ask for Gill Dold; or tel: (2712) 998-9989, Pretoria, South Africa. Secure camping sites; well-equipped, self-catering, 4-bed, thatched chalets.

WHERE TO EAT

Resort restaurants may only open only during peak periods (South African school holidays). Prepare to be self-catering – in the municipal markets of Maxixe and Inhambane's you will find a mouthwatering variety of fresh fish, fruit and vegetables, but be sure to bring processed foods with you.

Inhambane
Restaurante Tic Tic, 706 Av. da Revolução, Inhambane; no telephone. Very close to the Mercado Municipal; serves the best and cheapest fish and chips in the whole of East Africa.

Restaurante Prima Vera (Mariano's Bar), Av. Acordo de Lusaka, close to the jetty. Not to be missed, Senhor Mariano Armaro's establishment is open seven days a week from 08:00–24:00. His specialities are prawns, calamari and omelettes.

Tofo
Tofo Hotel, (see Where to Stay). Dine on delicious lobster while sitting on the cool front veranda.

Maxixe
Restaurante Dom Carlos, one block down from the main road, behind Golfinho Azul, tel: (23) 158. The best restaurant in town; prawns and calamari are a speciality.

Massinga
Restaurante Dalilo, located right next to one of the two filling stations, tel: (23) 3. Rashid, the owner, can proudly offer a selection of a dozen brands of ice-cold imported beer from his bar He also serves some very good soups, and a memorable (if a tad on the fiery side) piri-piri chicken.

SHOPPING

The Inhambane market has one of the best selections of colourful traditional arts and crafts in the country.

TOURS AND EXCURSIONS

Barra Lodge, in Ponta da Barra, (see Where to Stay), is able to arrange excursions to places of historical and natural interest. Scuba diving and courses and big game fishing are also available.
Morrungulo Marine Safaris, situated at the Morrungulo Dive Centre in Nelson's Bay (see Where to

Stay) offers dive courses along with full equipment and boat hire. A knowledgeable resident dive master gives single-day training sessions as well as the longer Open Water I (OW I) and OW II courses. A novel idea promoted by Marine Safaris is for guests to absolve their preliminary National Association of Underwater Instructors (**NAUI**) dive courses in Pretoria before departure. To contact the American-based dive school in Pretoria, South Africa, tel: (2712) 998-9989.
For some interesting beach outings in and around the Inhambane area, enquire at **Palms Bazar,** situated next door to the Mercado Central in Inhambane.

USEFUL CONTACTS

The only reliable contact in the Inhambane area is **Erwin Jakes** who not only possesses one of the preciously few operational telephones around here, but also speaks English, which makes him invaluable to the tourist. Furthermore, Erwin is able to arrange **boat launching permits** at short notice, but be sure to follow the correct procedures in order to avoid heavy fines, or worse, the confiscation of your craft. Erwin Jakes and Signorina, his sister-in-law, may be contacted at Maxixe, tel: (23) 2351.

5
Bazaruto Archipelago

Africa's version of the famed Galápagos Islands, the Bazaruto Archipelago and surrounding marine environment is a complex and unique ecosystem, well-protected by its isolation. Harbouring one of the last viable populations of dugong along the entire East African coast, the Bazarutos command some of the most pristine coral reefs in the Indian Ocean. In descending order of size **Bazaruto, Benguerra, Magaruque, Santa Carolina** and tiny undeveloped **Bangué Island** each have their own particular charm and character.

Amid the turquoise shallows surrounding each island, in the tidal inlets and shaded sea pastures opening into the deep Mozambique Channel, a wealth of marine life exists. For conservationists the uniqueness of this archipelago lies in its fragile diversity. Wildlife ranges from migrant bird species, **frigate birds** and **falcons** to **crocodiles** lurking in the brackish inland lakes. At least five species of **turtle** have their breeding ground here, while various **antelope**, rodents, lizards and snakes inhabit the massive mobile sand dunes and adjacent scrubland.

For the moment, only Bazaruto, Benguerra, and a narrow strip of adjacent sea have been designated as a national park. It is hoped that cooperation between the WWF International, Endangered Wildlife Trust, Southern African Nature Foundation, International Wilderness Leadership Foundation and South African Airways will lead to a sound conservation management policy, uniting all the islands under the protection of a greater 'Parque Nacional do Arquipélago do Bazaruto'.

DON'T MISS

*** **Bazaruto Archipelago:** excellent scuba diving and snorkelling on Two-Mile Reef.
*** **Fishing villages:** fascinating glimpse of village life.
*** **Charter cruises:** fabulous trips around the islands.
** **Big game fishing:** record-breaking catches of sailfish and barracuda.
** **Dhow day trips:** can be organized by lodges or dhows hired on the beach.
* **Baobab forests:** southernmost occurrence of these giant trees in Mozambique.

Opposite: *A fisherman carefully inspects his net at Benguerra Island.*

MAINLAND TOWNS
Vilankulo **

Located just about halfway between Mozambique's two largest cities (Maputo and Beira), Vilankulo has become an important public transport terminus. It lies only 21km (13 miles) off the EN1 and 10km (6 miles) away from **Magaruque Island**, which makes Magaruque that much more accessible from the mainland. An airport (direct international flights allowed) with a tarmac runway of 1300m (4300ft) serves the town. Taking this as well as the newly surfaced road into account, Vilankulo is fast becoming the mainland's gateway to the **Bazaruto Archipelago**. Developers are taking advantage of its location by opening lodges, camp sites, hotels, boat charters and restaurants. In addition, Vilankulo is well supplied by a central market, service stations, Indian shops and a medical clinic. Set up your tent or install yourself in one of the rustic huts, stock up on mandioca and lush papaya fruit and forget about shopping malls!

For a place to stay in Vilankulo it is advisable to get down to the **Hotel Dona Anna**, which overlooks the harbour, in order to orientate yourself. The hotel's shady veranda always offers a cool refuge from the heavy midday heat. From Hotel Dona Anna, turn right along the beach road. A short distance along you will find a revamped camp site which may have chalets operational by the time of your arrival. Backpackers

Opposite: *A boy from Vilankulo proudly shows off his unusual catch.*
Right: *This village near Vilankulo is close to the lovely beach.*

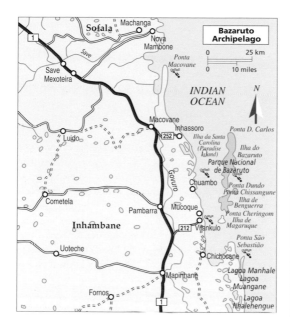

CONSERVATION

The community-oriented conservation and sustainable resource utilization programmes on **Bazaruto** and **Santa Carolina** are funded by the **Fundação Natureza em Perigo** (the Mozambique branch of the Endangered Wildlife Trust), the **World Wildlife Fund** and the **South African Nature Foundation**. Projects presently in progress include rehabilitation of the dune forests, educating the local population about their environment and studies of the elusive and rare dugong. Note: only tourists who are booked into one of the lodges are permitted to stay overnight on the islands (due to their protected status). Camp at your own peril.

and other independent travellers should ask for the **Casa de Senhor Josef**, a private reed-and-thatch home a little way past the **Quiosque Tropical**.

Still haven't found what you are looking for? Start again at the Dona Anna, and this time drive (or walk) to the left around the palm-lined bay, where small boats anchor and old ships are left to die. A sandy track leads past a few crumbling buildings, swings a little away from the beach, and heads out of town, still following the edge of the bay. Persist on this indistinct route (don't hesitate to ask locals, who will always tell you what they think you would like to know!) and you will reach two unassuming but charming little lodges, namely **Simbire Lodge** and (aptly named) **The Last Resort**.

The proprietor of **Bar Moçambicano** offers much more to the weary traveller than just good food and a friendly welcome; he can assist with accommodation, information, fishing and diving as well as general watersports, island boat cruises and provisions.

Right: *Magaruque Island Lodge offers accommodation in an idyllic setting.*
Opposite top: *A flock of flamingos sweeps in gracefully over Benguerra Island.*

Inhassoro *

Inhassoro is a small, sleepy **fishing village** 94km (58 miles) north of Vilankulo and 15km (9 miles) from the EN1. It does have a service station, but as the fuel pumps regularly run dry, don't rely on topping up your tank here. Inhassoro boasts a camp site, two hotels (*see* p. 86), a bus terminus, a handful of restaurants, general stores, a marketplace, a health post offering basic nursing service, a police station and a short grass airstrip a stone's throw away from the *bairros*. Inhassoro is not as yet linked up to the new phone system, but bookings can be made through HUTNIC in Tzaneen, South Africa.

THE ISLANDS
Ilha de Magaruque **

Circumnavigating Magaruque on foot is a leisurely three-hour stroll along deserted white beaches. In keeping with its postage-stamp proportions, the ambience of the island is relaxed and intimate. Magaruque Island Resort offers full board and lodging, and there is a choice of rooms, bungalows and chalets on offer.

Magaruque has the advantages of a paved airstrip, superb **snorkelling** or **scuba diving** on a coral reef just a short swim from the front of the hotel, and ease of accessibility from the mainland. Transfers in **ski-boats** to and from Vilankulo are available by prior arrangement, and there are always **dhow rides** for the adventurous.

ORGANIZAÇÕES JOAQUIM ALVES

Prior to the independence of Mozambique in 1975, **Senhor Joaquim Alves** of Vilankulo ran a small fleet of coasters, a chain of trading stores in the Vilankulo area, an air transport company and the **Hotel Dona Anna**, named after his wife. Senhor Alves also held the tourist concession for the entire Bazaruto Archipelago, and operated **Hotel Inhassoro** and the bungalows at the resort at **Bartolomeu Dias**, some 48km (28 miles) north of Inhassoro. The islands are now a national park, the hotels in need of repair, Bartolomeu Dias has slipped beneath the waves, and Senhor Alves would be about 100 years old, if alive today.

Ilha de Benguerra **

Since Benguerra is blessed with the most intact area of **indigenous dune forest** of all the islands, it probably offers the best **birding** as well. Freshwater lakes, surrounded by stunning golden dunes, are also populated by crocodiles which must already have been resident when the island separated from the mainland several thousand years ago. Apart from the shelters of a great many migratory fisherfolk who use Benguerra as a seasonal stopover, there are the **Benguerra Island Lodge** and the more rustic **Sabal Lodge**, as well as a convenient 800m-long (2625ft) airstrip.

Ilha da Santa Carolina (Paradise Island) **

Pérola do Indico, 'Pearl of the Indian Ocean' the Portuguese called it, but it will always be **Paradise Island** to those who have enjoyed its isolation.

About 3km (2 miles) long and roughly 500m (547yd) wide, from the air the tiny island resembles an athletics track. The 100-room **hotel** was derelict for decades, but the ever optimistic staff offered visiting yachtspeople a meal on the veranda, and talked of a time when their *padrão*, or former Portuguese boss, would finally return. The most recent developments on Paradise involve the partial restoration of the hotel and various facilities. Visitors can arrange to arrive by air from Johannesburg or Maputo, or by boat from Vilankulo or Inhassoro.

> **SAND DUNES SURROUNDED BY SEA**
>
> The three larger islands (Bazaruto, Benguerra and Magaruque) were once joined, forming a 70km (42-mile) sand spit moulded by a combination of wind action, changing sea levels and long-shore current drift. This giant sand dune broke into four bits some 6000 years ago (Santa Carolina, a rocky outcrop, had separated from the mainland 120,000 years previously). Only Santa Carolina is a true rock island surrounded by deeper water – better boat anchorage than Benguerra and Bazaruto. Magaruque has a deep channel near the lodge but, with a tidal range of 4m (13ft), low tide leaves most of its beaches a long way from the sea.

Left: *Tourists on the* Kingfisher *fish the blue waters around Benguerra.*

FAROL DO BAZARUTO

Built by the Portuguese in 1890, this **paraffin-powered lighthouse** is just one of a string that guided mariners through the treacherous waters of the **Mozambique Channel**. Lighthouses were supplied, on an irregular basis, by a small ship which steamed up and down the Mozambican coastline and sent out a rowboat with supplies. Like many others, Farol do Bazaruto was in a sad state of disrepair, but its rehabilitation formed part of an ambitious expansion project undertaken by the Bazaruto Island Lodge owners.

Ilha do Bazaruto★★★

About 30km (18 miles) long and some 3km (2 miles) at its widest, Bazaruto is the biggest island in the archipelago. Parallel with the mainland, on its northern point where the Farol do Bazaruto (lighthouse) last flashed out to sea 20 years ago, there is tourist accommodation in the form of the **Bazaruto Island Lodge**.

The island is served by a grass airstrip capable of handling light aircraft. In the event of the strip becoming almost impossible to land on (which sometimes happens after one of the rare thunderstorms), you would land on Magaruque's paved runway instead and be transferred to your destination by boat. You will have to beach some distance from the lodge if you don't happen to arrive at high tide, but will be taken to the lodge by Land-Rover.

Island Fishing ★★★

Bazaruto Island, as well as Benguerra and Magaruque, are attracting increasing numbers of saltwater fly fishermen and -women; the sight of someone standing etched against a golden sunrise, gracefully casting their line out over the waves, is a vision as ancient as the sand itself.

Crossbars on which catches of the day could be hung up, weighed and photographed once formed a focal point of the island experience but are rarely used nowadays. Today's environmentally friendly fishers prefer to weigh, photograph and tag their trophies before releasing them alive and kicking back into the blue. Conservation and rehabilitation of the environment is uppermost in the minds of lodge owners and management who are campaigning to have the archipelago declared a World Heritage Site.

Of added interest to nature lovers are the southern lakes which are inhabited by **freshwater crocodiles** and a few elusive species of endemic butterfly.

Below: *Many fishermen visit Bazaruto Island in the hope of landing the Big One.*

Left: *Although many land-mines have been cleared throughout Mozambique, they remain a potential hazard and motorists are advised not to veer onto unknown tracks.*

EN ROUTE TO BEIRA

Most motorists from South Africa don't travel further north than Vilankulo. In the past this was due to the poor condition of the EN1 between Vilankulo and Beira, as well as a lack of important facilities such as service stations and accommodation. Times have changed; the EN1 has been resurfaced as far north as **Rio Save** and there are **fuel stations** at the turnoff to **Inhassoro**, at **Rio Save** as well as at **Inchope**. Although most maps claim that fuel is available at **Mapinhane** this is not currently the case. Mapinhane does, however, deserve a mention as it is a pretty little town with basic (truckers') accommodation and food at **Restaurante Boa Viagem**.

Apart from the EN1, **minor roads** in the coastal area between Inhassoro and Beira have not yet been upgraded, and may become impassable during the November to March rains. There are many river crossings, and ferries may not be operational, while forgotten **landmines** will remain a hazard for some time to come. Hire a local guide, who knows all the tricky areas, to show you around.

Even though **Sofala** is one of the country's oldest settlements, visitors anticipating being able to scramble among romantic ancient ruins will be disappointed. Shifting sand dunes have obliterated the site of the former fort, but the unspoilt beach is charming enough to attract self-sufficient sun-seekers and fishermen.

SOFALA, ANCIENT OPHIR OF THE BIBLE?

Known to Arab sailors since biblical times, reference to **Sofala** is made in Milton's epic *Paradise Lost*. Desperate to boost their lagging economy, the Portuguese crown embarked upon a frenzied search for what it believed to be the legendary golden city of **Ophir**. In 1501 the Portuguese established a permanent presence at Sofala. Apart from a few gold beads, though, the treasure trove did not materialize and the surviving settlers returned home empty-handed. During 1904 stone from Sofala's old fort was used to build a cathedral in **Beira** – an apparent act of vandalism until one realizes that the ancient site was being obliterated by wave erosion to such an extent that today there isn't a trace left of the fort's foundations.

MIOMBO WOODLAND

North of the **Rio Save** the EN1 cuts through wild unspoilt **miombo** (*Brachystegia* sp.) **woodland**. The entire length of the journey is lined with towering **msasa** (*Brachystegia spiciformis*) and **mufuti** (*Brachystegia boehmii*), capable of reaching heights of 20m (65ft). Home to many birds (rollers, barbets, woodpeckers, eagles), the **brachystegia woodland** in southern Africa is confined to Mozambique south of the Zambezi, most of Zimbabwe and the southern quarter of Malawi. **Cattle farming** is a potential threat to these forests as ranchers often remove trees to promote the growth of food grasses.

POTHOLES (COVAS) AND TRENCHES (TRINCHEIRAS)

A good indication of potholes or trenches ahead is patches of sand on both sides of the tarmac road. Verges are not cleared of grass, so wherever vehicles go around an obstacle, they kill the vegetation, leaving telltale gouges in the bush. This applies to many other roads in Mozambique, particularly those in the Zambezia, Nampula and Cabo Delgado provinces.

Nova Mambone *

Accessible via a very poor track from **Mexoteira** on the EN1, 18km (11 miles) south of the Save River, Mambone is the **prawn capital** of Mozambique. Silt carried down by the **Rio Save** as well as the mangrove swamps in the area provide an ideal breeding ground for the crustaceans. Mambone is not often visited by travellers, but a *pensão* (boarding house) and very basic restaurant are ready to receive guests. If you do venture to these shores, bring along a boat – the mouth of the Save is a fascinating place to explore.

Save River Bridge *

To cross over the Save River bridge you have to pay a small toll. Also have your vehicle papers and driver's licence ready as police may want to examine these here. Stop to buy a few fresh bread rolls and cold drinks, and relax in the shade overlooking the beautiful river valley. The 258km (160-mile) stretch between **Save** and **Inchope** (on the EN6 between Beira and Mutare in Zimbabwe) is lonely, remote and beautiful. Apart from the odd logging camp where you might find water and diesel (at a price), don't expect any facilities.

The condition of the road surface is so poor in places that locals refer to those parts as *via a pé* (footway), because only pedestrians can pick their way along the middle – motorists are forced to make detours. However, the road is due for upgrading shortly.

When using this route, common sense dictates that you travel in a convoy of two or more cars, carry extra fuel and a comprehensive set of vehicle spares such as fan belts, radiator hoses, fuses and a puncture repair kit. Also, be sure to depart early in the morning, as night-driving on pot-holed surfaces can be very dangerous.

Espungabera to the Coast *

The only west–east route feasible in central Mozambique south of Beira is the wild, scenic and rugged track which begins at the **Mt Selinda–Espungabera frontier** with Zimbabwe (open 09:00–16:00).

The first 105km (66 miles) to the ramshackle town of **Dombe** traverse the southernmost reaches of the beautiful sandstone **Chimanimani mountain range** where you may come across leopard, eland and baboon. The **Lucite River-crossing** at Dombe may require some care and preparation (such as the plugging of gear boxes and differential breathing-holes) during the December to April rains, as the low-level bridge may be flooded then.

From Dombe the track winds alongside the lazy Lucite River for 60km (37 miles) until it intersects with the much wider EN1. If you have sufficient fuel to cover a further 400km (250 miles), sticking strictly to the well-used course for fear of landmines, cross the main road and continue on the final 120km (75 miles) parallel to the Búzi River, through Goonda and Nova Almada to the village of Búzi . This is an important agricultural centre which is served by motorized ferries from Beira on an irregular basis, but usually about twice a week. Some of your party could take the ferry to Beira, while the driver reaches the city via Inchope. The boat-trippers can be collected at the small **Mananga boat harbour** in the *baixa*, adjacent to the historic building of the Manica Beira company.

> ### MAGICAL MUSIC OF THE MBIRA
>
> Andrew Tracey, Professor of African Music at South Africa's Rhodes University in Grahamstown, has visited the area between the Búzi and Save rivers in search of the enchanting tunes played by the **Ndau people** on their mbiras. The mbira is a small wooden instrument with metal keys. Played with the thumb and index finger, it produces a sound similar to that of a tiny tin harp. Some of Mozambique's most influential mbira virtuosos hail from the **Machanga** region (to the north of the Save's mouth) and the adjacent offshore islands of **Nyanguwo** and **Chiloane**.

Left: *Tired after a long day's hike, these backpackers are glad to reach the relative safety of this overnight shelter in the Chimanimani mountain range.*

Bazaruto Archipelago at a Glance

BEST TIMES TO VISIT

The beaches in this area are usually cooled by **sea breezes** which moderate the weather somewhat. Best avoided perhaps are November to March when average monthly **rainfall** is above 200mm (8in) and the combination of **high temperatures** (35°C; 95°F) and 100% **humidity** can make conditions uncomfortable.

GETTING THERE

All of the islands have airstrips which are served daily by **charter companies** (see p. 42). **Vilankulo** has a small airport of entry suitable for large turboprop aircraft. **Inhassoro**'s short bumpy strip is only used by daring 'bush pilots'. At present there are no scheduled flights to these destinations, but fly-in **package tours** may be arranged. Both Vilankulo and Inhassoro are only a few minutes away from the EN1, which is in good condition from Maputo, but still under construction from Beira.

GETTING AROUND

Both Transportes Oliveiras and Transportes Virginias **buses** service the area and **dhows** (for adventurous folk who have unlimited time) sail between Inhambane and Vilankulo and from Vilankulo to Inhassoro and the islands. **Speedboat** and **dhow**

transfers by are available between the archipelago and Inhassoro or Vilankulo. *Chapas* operate between the mainland towns, and dhows sail up and down the coast between the coastal towns and the islands. No car hire facilities are available in this area. Please note: hitchhikers accepting lifts on transport trucks will be expected to pay for the journey.

WHERE TO STAY

Vilankulo
MID-RANGE
Hotel Dona Anna, book a call and ask for 'Vilankulo 21'. It appears as though the managers of this hotel change regularly; expect reasonable food and beds.

BUDGET
Simbire Lodge, no telephone. Accommodation is in traditional 2-bed huts (no linen); cheap camping; showers come in a bucket; feast on *matapas* and fresh fish.

Inhassoro
MID-RANGE
Hotel Seta, tel: (27152) 4284, Tzaneen, South Africa. One of the most secure and peaceful places in the country with a dining–entertaining complex and a pub panelled in hardwoods; mahogany trees shade a breezy patio overlooking the beach; six self-contained chalets (each with two double bedrooms

and bathroom en-suite), as well as a treed camping area with excellent ablution facilities are available.

Complexo Salema Mufundisse Chibique, tel: (1) 72-2846 (Maputo), or book a call and ask for 'Inhassoro 12'. Mainly used by local travellers.

Bazaruto Island
LUXURY
Bazaruto Island Lodge, tel: (2711) 447-3528, fax: 880-5364, Johannesburg, South Africa or Pestana Hotels in Maputo, tel: (01) 42- 0525, fax: 42-0524. The lodge overlooks a small coral-fringed, palm-lined bay across which Ilha Santa Carolina is an indistinct dot and the mainland just a shimmering blur. Accommodation is in luxurious A-frame chalets with a beautiful backdrop of forest-covered sand dunes and the century-old lighthouse. No effort is spared to enchant the clients.

MID-RANGE
Sabal Lodge, tel/fax: (2711) 888-3168, Johannesburg, South Africa. A new lodge offering affordable fishing.

Benguerra Island
LUXURY
Benguela Lodge, contact Benguela Island Holidays in Johannesburg, South Africa,

Bazaruto Archipelago at a Glance

tel: (2711) 483-2734/5, fax: 728-3767; or in Maputo, tel/fax: (1) 3-2846.
Central dining area, a swimming pool and 13 thatched bungalows tucked underneath the canopy of an indigenous forest.

Marlin Lodge, tel: (2712) 543-2134, fax: 543-2135, Pretoria, South Africa. Superb facilities and Caribbean ambience.

Magaruque Island
MID-RANGE
Magaruque Island Lodge, tel: (2634) 79-6411, fax: 70-6148, Harare, Zimbabwe or book through PROSOL, tel: (01) 2-9606 or 3-4096 or SABINAIR, tel: (01) 46-5108, both in Maputo. Comfortable and affordable accommodation – far less expensive than the other exclusive island lodges.

WHERE TO EAT

All of the island resorts and lodges offer a full-board service. Forget that diet before you arrive – the food is both healthy and scrumptious.

Vilankulo
Quiosque Tropical, offers simple but tasty fare.

Inhassoro
Hotel Seta (*see Where to Stay*). Meals on offer at this restaurant range from fish with chips and fresh salad to prawns and coconut rice. Be sure to give the chef ample notice (one or two hours) before you wish to eat.

SHOPPING

As is the case in the rest of the country, the municipal markets are the cheapest and most interesting places to shop. Undoubtedly, one of the main culinary attractions of this area is the colourful array of tropical and deciduous fruit that is available. December to March is good for mangoes, papayas, pineapples, bananas and avocado pears, while June to September is the season for oranges, *naartjies* (tangerines), tomatoes and corn-on-the-cob. Coconuts are available all year round.

TOURS AND EXCURSIONS

Guests at any of the island lodges will be able to amuse themselves with a full range of interesting watersports including **sail-boarding, snorkelling, waterskiing** and **scuba diving**
Day trips by motorlaunch from Magaruque, Bazaruto and Benguerra to scenic Vilankulo town and its bustling market can also be arranged. For further information contact the respective lodges (*see Where to Stay*).
Marine Safaris Mozambique, tel: (2712) 998-9989, Pretoria, South Africa. This company offer luxurious cruises among the beautiful islands of the Bazaruto Archipelago on a fully equipped 11m (36ft) dive catamaran. Day trips from Benguerra island or Vilankulo can be arranged too. For various **outings from the islands** contact the respective island's booking office, or book the tours upon your arrival. Alternatively, it is possible to organize your very own expedition from Vilankulo or Inhassoro. Speak to one of the **dhow** owners down on the beach to make the necessary arrangements. But do take note: beware of sudden gusty storms, especially during the cyclone or typhoon season which lasts from December to April.

USEFUL CONTACTS

Although Vilankulo and Inhassoro are linked to the outside world by telephone, calls can only be made via the **international operator**. The more common means of communication in this area is the radio (contact the resort booking offices for frequencies).
Empresa Nacional de Turismo, the National Tourism company, can be contacted in Maputo, tel: (01) 42-5011/3 or tel: (2711) 339-7275, Johannesburg.
Pestana Hotels and Resorts, Maputo, tel: (1) 42-7372, fax: 42-0524; or Johannesburg, tel: (2711) 447-6499, fax: 799-6499.

6
From Beira to Tete

Beira (capital of Sofala province) and Tete (capital of Tete) are the largest towns in Mozambique's central and western region respectively. Both are historically and architecturally fascinating, owing their existence to the need for trading outlets: **Tete** is a Zambezi River port and **Beira** a busy ocean harbour at the mouth of the Púngoè River. Tete's two squat sandstone stockades reveal its former 'frontier town' status, while dhows, handcrafted a stone's throw away, still ply Beira's ultramodern docks.

In this region the Mozambican Plain narrows, giving way to the Mozambican Plateau and the **Chimanimani**, **Gorongosa** and **Bvumba mountain ranges**. Mangrove swamps still occur sporadically along the coast, but corals are restricted by the shallows produced by a widening continental shelf as well as the influence of silt deposited at the mouths of the Búzi, Púngoè and Zambezi rivers.

Mozambique's most extensive **mangrove swamps** occur between Beira and Nova Mambone, and around Quelimane. For birders this habitat is significant – it harbours rare species like the **palmnut vulture** and elusive **mangrove kingfisher**, found in greater numbers here than anywhere else on earth.

The once world-famous **Gorongosa National Park** has reached an advanced stage of restoration and can currently accommodate casual visitors who are able to fend for themselves. Vast herds of elephant, buffalo and other wildlife are being reintroduced and the park's original boundaries extended to ensure that the raw romance of Africa retains its tenuous grip on this region.

DON'T MISS

*** Praça do Município: enjoy an espresso in this historical square.
*** Johnny's Place: the oldest restaurant in town.
*** Mercado Municipal: shop here for tropical fruit.
** Macúti Beach: fascinating shipwreck and lighthouse.
** Bique's: restaurant and chalets on Macúti Beach.
* Makonde sculptures: lovely Mozambican artworks.
* Lambada: dance at **Centro Hípico** or **Clube Oceana**.

Opposite: *En route to Cahora Bassa you will come across many traditional villages like this one.*

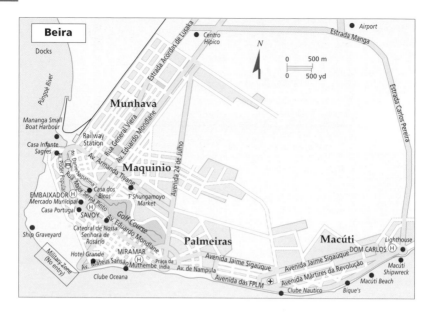

BEIRA

A fairly large, important port city situated at the mouth of the Púngoè River about halfway up the country's coast, Beira is Mozambique's second city after Maputo.

Beira's origins lie in the historic settlement of **Sofala** which is a short dhow trip down the coast. Sofala was an Arab trading outpost for hundreds of years, where gold, ivory and slaves were exchanged for Arab cloth and dyes, beads and spices. About 500 years later, Portuguese navigators, including Vasco da Gama, sailed into the estuary formed by the Rio Púngoè, to see if there was any truth in the story that gold was to be found in Sofala. It was not until 1887, when the European powers began their colonial expansion into Africa, that the site was considered important enough for the Portuguese to establish a military garrison. Coincidentally, the Portuguese crown prince Dom Luis Filipe, who was born at roughly the same time, was given the title Prince of Beira. The new settlement was named in his honour.

Then the British, desperately seeking a sea outlet for their landlocked possession, southern Rhodesia, cast their eyes upon Beira. The British 'Chartered Company' troops clashed with Portuguese soldiers on a number of occasions in this area, while at the same time Portuguese traders began to explore Lake Malawi. Hostilities were finally ended with the signing of the **Anglo-Portuguese Treaty** of 1891, which, at last, defined the political boundaries of modern Mozambique and her neighbours.

During this period, the town of Beira was nothing but a stinking, fever-ridden mangrove estuary where malaria and dysentery ruled. Most of the early residents braved disease in search of their fortune during the frantic 'Manica gold rush'. Governor General Enes is recorded as saying of the new arrivals: 'Ten or twelve pounds a month was paid in order to live, baked by slow heat between sheets of galvanized iron . . . a visitor to the taverns of Beira, could hear veritable concerts of curses and blasphemies from the disillusioned, calling down fire from Heaven upon those who had deceived them with false hopes of wealth'.

PRAÇA DO MUNICÍPIO

Since most buildings around the Praça do Município date from the colonial era, visitors may feel as though they were in the south of Portugal. During the day, the **municipal square** with its large central water feature, and **municipal offices**, which have a marble mural of the old Sofala fort in the hallway, are the social focal point for Beira's more affluent residents. Surrounded by **coffee shops** with tables under the trees on the pavement, the praça's ambience is more European than African.

Below: *The busy harbour of Beira is port of call for a variety of vessels.*

T'SHUNGAMOYO

T'Shungamoyo means courage in the local **Ndau** dialect. Whether the informal markets in Beira reflect a brave attempt at prosperity or allude to their precarious legal status, the markets are referred to as T'Shungamoyo. The lively **Mercado do Goto** is a colourful sprawl of stalls selling *capulanas*, clothing, motor spares and electrical goods. Should the crowded chaos prove to daunting, a more tame market to explore is the **Mercado Municipal** in central Beira, the town's original colonial market.

Opposite: *The old-world charm of the Casa Portugal in Beira is captivating.*
Below: *The ferry at Caia is a vital mode of transport across the Zambezi River.*

The first impression on arriving in the *bairro* Maquinino on the city's outskirts may not be very favourable, but once you get over it, Beira holds hidden rewards for the inquisitive visitor. Beira is drab, dirty and chaotic, but it is also bewitching. Although the city is a lot smaller than Maputo, it was strategically far more important than the national capital during the civil war period (1977–92) due to its central location.

Beira's buildings display a mixture of colonial excess, bland post-war American and constrained socialist functionality in addition to the tin, cardboard and reed shelters of rampant unplanned urbanization.

The imposing **Railway Station** overlooks Praça dos Trabalhadores, where the parking space available far outstrips demand, although trains do the journey between Beira and Zimbabwe twice a week. The railway entrance hall has a high, curved ceiling, and an ornamental fish pond. Overlooking this echoing, empty space is a clean and cool restaurant with an interesting menu and wine list.

A walk along the beachfront reveals what will become an enormous challenge to future city engineers: the sea is gradually undermining Beira's foundations.

Beira's Architecture ★★★

The beautiful **Catedral de Nossa Senhora de Rosário** (Cathedral of Our Lady of the Rosary) on Avenida Eduardo Mondlane was commissioned in 1907 and completed in 1915. Stone from the old Portuguese fort at Sofala was used in its construction. Services are held every day.

The **Clube des Chinês** building, erected in 1917, was designed in the neoclassical style. Once renovations are completed it will again be one of Beira's finest structures. Originally a club for Chinese settlers, it now houses the city archives.

The quaint **Casa Portugal** (Portugal House) with its tin roof, is a private residence located off Praça do Metical next to the **Banco Standard Totta**, and is typical of the turn-of-the-century colonial period.

Its high stone walls topped with battlements, the **Prisão da Beira** (Beira prison) resembles a medieval castle. It lies just off Praça do Metical and is still in use today. Family members of the prisoners bring food to the inmates on a daily basis.

Don't miss the avant-garde exhibition hall named **Casa dos Bicos** after the sharp points on its roof (*bico* means beak or point) located on Av. Eduardo Mondlane.

Near the old golf course, on the way to the Praça da India, the Cinema São Jorge seats 1200 people and is one of the largest and most ornate cinemas in Africa.

Be sure to look at the **Casa Infante Sagres** on the west end of Avenida Poder Popular. This neoclassical building now houses the Manica Mozambique company that was responsible for its renovation.

Mananga Small Boat Harbour ★★

Small wooden fishing vessels and ancient, rusting trawlers rub shoulders with each other here. More than just a safe place to anchor, this is a floating village housing a special community of honest fishermen.

> **THE LATE, GREAT, GRAND HOTEL**
>
> When it was erected near the mouth of the Púngoè in 1952, the **Hotel Grande** was Beira's most impressive structure. Today, sadly, it is a derelict high-rise squatter camp where goats meet you at the entrance and trees grow from balconies. Urban legend has it that, at independence, the hotel was handed over to the people by the socialist government, but this is not the case. From the outset, the hotel's tariffs were too high and too few wealthy tourists visited Beira to make it pay. The Grande has not received any guests since 1963, 12 years before Frelimo assumed power.

Art Galleries **

There are quite a few interesting art galleries around. Visit the fashionable **Atelier Canheze**, which has more expensive works for sale; the **Coroas de Moçambique**, which has a fascinating range of traditional musical instruments as well as some beautiful hardwood sculptures available; there is also the **Co-operative Artesanato 25 de Marco**, which specializes in commissioned works of art; the **Sociedade de Escultures 25 de Setembro**, where sculptors sit and chip away at wood and ivory outside their shacks; and the **Casa da Cultura**, a theatre-restaurant that, on the odd occasion, hosts exhibitions.

Mercado Municipal ***

The municipal market, just a few paces away from Praça do Município, is one of Mozambique's most colourful and best-stocked marketplaces. Fruit and vegetables arrive by the truckload from as far afield as Maputo, Quelimane and Malawi, while dhows and chugging trawlers bring in fish, prawns, calamari and other food from the sea. Tiny stalls sell anything from toothbrushes to tinned tuna, and many splendid local crafts such as figurines in *pau-preto* (ebony) and *pau-rosa* (mahogany) are also on offer. Have you ever dreamed of mangoes the size of footballs, bananas as big as your forearm, and pineapples too heavy to pick up with one hand? At Beira's Mercado Municipal that fantasy may become a reality!

Macúti Beach, Shipwreck and Lighthouse **

The *bairro* of Macúti, one of Beira's wealthier residential areas, is named after a trawler that was wrecked nearby during a cyclone in 1917. It appears ironic that the skeleton of the *Macúti* should have ended right beneath the lighthouse that was supposed to lead it to safety, but the hull was, in fact, towed there to act as a breakwater. Macúti beach extends some distance to the north and south of the lighthouse, and it is here that Beira's residents come to swim and promenade on weekends. Walk up past the lighthouse to where gaily painted wooden fishing boats lie hull up and the fishermen lay out their nets for repair. This is the best place to buy Beira's famous **prawns**, as well as a mouthwatering variety of other fresh seafood. The lighthouse is in good condition, and still accommodates the keeper and his family.

Take a look at the **Dom Carlos Hotel** behind the lighthouse, which was Beira's five-star flagship before independence but is now deserted except for a few loyal staff. Although the building is crumbling, the hotel's personnel have been waiting patiently for 20 years for the return of their boss. They will welcome you, if you don't mind the lack of running water and electricity and don't believe in the ghosts that are said to haunt the premises.

A word of warning: only venture out in groups after dark, as muggings have become a problem in this area.

Opposite: *Beira's Praça do Município is just a few paces away from the market.* **Below:** *The Macúti was towed in front of the lighthouse to form a breakwater.*

Right: *These Shona women are crossing a bridge over the Púngoè River on their way home.*
Below: *A gifted Makonde sculptor carves away at his next work of art.*

The Ship Graveyard **

From Praça do Município, walk west in the direction of the Púngoè River, past an informal market which specializes in selling clothes. On your left there will be warehouses and beyond them a large open area which must be avoided as it is a **military zone** (*zona militar*). Walk into the informal scattering of thatch-and-reed huts and watch out for the rusty steel prow of a ship sticking up from the shore of the river. Vessels that had been sabotaged by the Rhodesian Special Air Service in 1977 or had sunk due to being unseaworthy have been towed here and abandoned.

Not only is this ship graveyard a monument to the follies of war and bankrupt socialist policies – it is also an amazing photo opportunity. Don't wave around your camera, though, as it could be stolen. Nearby you can see wooden ships being built according to ancient designs.

Makonde Sculptors *

Sculptors from the fiercely independent Makonde tribe of Cabo Delgado province have set up a small co-operative where Av. Martíres de Revolução meets Av. das FPLM. Their small run-down shack has a storeroom and a showroom where statues, traditional weapons and musical instruments are displayed. Much of the artists' work has been toned down to suit the taste of tourists – the real Makonde art is characteristically bizarre and surreal.

Left: *These eerie-looking masks were fashioned by Makonde artists.*

Lambada Dancing *

One of the more colourful and frivolous legacies of the Portuguese period in Mozambique's history is that of Latin-American dancing (a favourite with the temperamental, fun-loving Portuguese) which is popular at some nightspots. From 21:00 onwards, one of the places to be in Beira is the **Clube Oceana** in Av. Mateus Sansão Muthemba, on the beachfront halfway between Praça da India and the derelict Grande Hotel.

For a slightly younger vibe, take your dancing shoes to the **Centro Hípico**, situated where the airport road meets the highway to Dondo, Chimoio, Manica and Zimbabwe.

Savane River and Rio Maria *

Located about 40km (25 miles) to the north of Beira on the Savane River is the little village of Rio Maria. This was once a holiday resort (and perhaps will be again in the future), but at present visitors have to be completely self-sufficient.

Due to the rather sandy track, it is recommended that only 4WD vehicles attempt the drive through this scenic patch of indigenous forest which has somehow survived the rigours of logging and the thoughtless destruction of slash-and-burn farming. Coming from Macúti, the road to Rio Maria branches off from the airport road just before the military barracks and airport terminal buildings. Get there before the loggers do!

> **THE STRIPED WATER DOG**
>
> *Hydrocynus vittatus* translates as 'striped water dog' but is known to countless fishermen as the **tiger fish**. Its Latin name is apt – it roams fresh tropical waters, attacking lesser fish. The tiger is lord of central Africa's inland waterways, but it is this contempt for invaders that is its undoing. Man, with rod and artificial lures, casts the bait into the tiger's territory and the aggressive predator attacks without reserve. Once hooked, the fish erupts into a sprint near the water's surface, broken by leaps into the air as it attempts to rid itself of the irritation. Once a fisherman has had a fighting tiger on the end of his line it is not only the 'water dog' that is hooked!

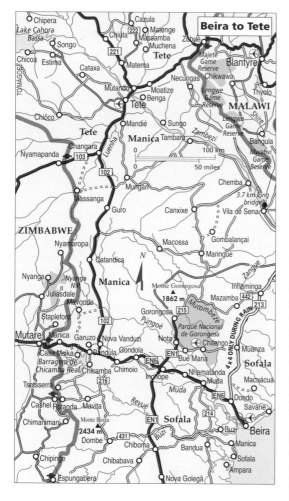

EN ROUTE TO TETE

In an effort to decrease Mozambique's dependence on South Africa's infrastructure, roads between Beira and Chimoio (192km; 119 miles), and Chimoio to Tete (389km; 241 miles) were the first to be rehabilitated. The former impetus (apartheid in South Africa; civil war in Mozambique) may have disappeared, but the road surface remains in **good condition**.

As in most of central and northern Mozambique, fuel and repair facilities are scarce, but there are service stations in Beira, Chimoio, Catandica and Tete. Please note that driving at night is not recommended, because of domestic and wild animals crossing the road, and stationary trucks parked hazardously along the way.

If you wish to head for **Zambezia province** in the north, you will have to drive to **Caia** via Dondo, just out of Beira on the EN6. Here there is a service station and a **control point**, but only cargo trucks are required to pull over for a customs check. As in all built-up areas, assume that the speed limit is 30kph (19mph) and drive accordingly or risk a hefty spot-fine. A short distance out of **Dondo** take the turnoff right onto the EN213 which, in places, is in a very poor state as far as Caia, but is undergoing repair.

Opposite: *Chitengo camp in the Gorongosa National Park is once again able to receive visitors.*

Gorongosa National Park ★★★

The little town of Gorongosa is located close to its name-sake, the Gorongosa National Park. It lies off the route from Beira to Tete at the terminus of the EN1, which will one day extend into the provinces north of the Zambezi.

Visits to the once-famous park are possible once more: landmines have been lifted, fences re-erected and some game reintroduced. For inside information on where to spot wildlife seek the local English-speaking crowd who congregate at **Bique's** (pronounced 'Beeky's') on Macúti Beach. Senhor Chande, the game warden in charge of rehabilitation, has set up basic facilities for visitors at **Chitengo camp**. Note though, that you'll have to be fully self-sufficient during your stay and that most of the Gorongosa's tracks become impassable from December to May due to flooding.

Chimoio ★

Once a resort for wealthy Beira residents, now a farming centre, Chimoio has mild winters and warm summers. Two service stations on the bypass off the EN6 are able to offer repairs and very limited spares. Chimoio also has banks, a post office, a library, a museum, a central market, supermarkets and telephones that work! Weary travellers can hang up their battered boots at the **Motel Moinho**, named after its mill-shaped reception area.

GORONGOSA'S WILDLIFE

Of the Big Five only elephant and buffalo are commonly spotted by visitors. Rhino and leopard also occur, but are exceptionally human-shy due to past poaching. Lions, were mercilessly hunted during the past strife, but are making a comeback and are often found slinking around their old haunt, *casa dos leões*, the ruins of the original rest camp. Herds of rare sable and roan ante-lope, zebra, impala, kudu and eland, as well as the odd elu-sive cheetah also roam across the park's vast expanse. The Gorongosa's birdlife could well be labelled the 'little five hundred' as this is approximately the number of species occuring in the area.

DR LIVINGSTONE, I PRESUME

The famous missionary and explorer Dr David Livingstone had left the shores of west Africa in 1854 on a mission to claim territory for God and for Queen Victoria. After visit-ing the falls on the Zambezi River which he named after his monarch, he vanished for months and was feared dead. In 1856 he emerged from the bush, haggard and ill, and was welcomed by the Portuguese at **Tete**, where he spent a few months convalescing. During this time he explored the area and noted the existence of surface coal diggings and alluvial gold panning.

BALANCING ROCKS

Millions of years ago, immense pools of molten silica, magnesium, iron and other minerals and metals, thrust close to the earth's surface by tectonic forces, began to cool. Surface forces of water, waves, wind and ice gradually scraped away the covering layers until the now solid granite batholiths and laccoliths became exposed in places. Expansion due to decreasing pressure had caused deep, uniform cracks which were now widened by chemical and mechanical weathering processes. Along sections of the **Catandica–Changara** road these formations resemble immense building blocks piled high by a playful giant.

CHICAMBA REAL DAM

Heading towards Zimbabwe on the EN6, skirt Chimoio and carry on past the turnoff to **Changara** and Tete from where the turnoff to the dam wall is a further 13km (8 miles). A good gravel road turns right up a steep hill and passes through picturesque little **Chicamba village** where you can stock up on fruit, vegetables and dried fish. From a vantage point near the dam control room you have unimpeded **views** of the entire dam. See if you can spot the lodge and crocodile farm at Casa Msika, on the opposite bank.

Barragem de Chicamba Real (Chicamba Real dam) is built on the confluence of the Revué and Msika rivers. Until local residents returned from refugee camps in Zimbabwe and netted the lake's fish, record-breaking bass and carp were being caught by sport fishermen from South Africa and Zimbabwe. Nevertheless, a fishing competition is still held annually during September.

From the top of the hill, follow the road down to the river. Cross it and you will see the 125m (410ft) concrete wall on your right. From here the road leads out of the small valley to the water's edge where you will find an enterprising fellow operating a **restaurant** and *quiosque* from a converted ocean transport container. A short distance behind this unusual roadhouse lies a makeshift parking area. Here you'll be able to launch a boat (with a little help from the locals), although a better **launching site** lies on the opposite side of the lake at Casa Msika.

About 50km (31 miles) from Chimoio, and 18km (11 miles) if you are coming from the direction of Manica, the turnoff to **Casa Msika** is marked by a clearly painted sign on a stone wall. Stay over at the comfortable lodge or camp site, have a chat to the fascinating owner, Peter Thornicroft, paddle on the lake or fish for

Below: *Villagers, like this woman in Chimoio, still live in mud-and-straw huts.*

Left: *En route to the Cahora Bassa dam in Tete province, the traveller will encounter many traditional villages.*

bass, visit the crocodile farm and take a walk through the bird-rich miombo (*Brachystegia* sp.) woodland. The beaches of Lake Chicamba, dotted with the skeletons of dead trees, are eerily scenic.

From the Estrada Nacional there is a turnoff north to Changara and Tete. It is another 62km (38 miles) to a quite rickety wood-and-steel bridge over the Rio Púngoè, and then a further 60km (37 miles) to the small town of **Catandica**, where you will be are able to refuel and purchase a few refreshments at the little store.

Changara lies 485km (301 miles) from Beira and 95km (59 miles) from Tete at the junction of **Estrada 102** and **Estrada 103**, which formed part of the infamous Tete Corridor of the war years. There is no operational service station at Changara at present.

SONGO AND LAKE CAHORA BASSA

About 128km (79½ miles) upstream from Tete, the beautiful Kebrabassa rapids thundered unhindered through an almost inaccessible gorge. As early as 1957, when Mozambique was still a province of Portugal, a commission investigating the development potential of the Zambezi River valley recommended the construction of a dam for irrigation purposes and flood control. Kebrabassa was the site chosen, and plans for a formidable hydroelectric power station were finalized in 1960. On-site accommodation and amenities

MSIKA HOUSE

. Hard times often serve to develop qualities of resilience, adaptability and ingenuity. Ex-Zimbabwean **Peter Thornicroft** found himself trying to survive in the midst of Mozambique's post-independence struggles, and excelled. Gaining a concession to farm on the shores of undeveloped **Chicamba Real**, Peter began to exploit the thousands of crocodiles that inhabit the lake. With meat at a premium due to devastated cattle herds, 'Senhor Crocodilos' as he was nicknamed by his staff, obtained a government contract to supply crocodile meat to the troops guarding the Beira Corridor. More recently he has built a tourist lodge, **Casa Msika**, which caters for international visitors seeking to fish the ample stocks of bass and bream, as well as Beira business people on a weekend's escape from the steamy humidity of the coast.

were urgently needed for the hundreds of workers, engineers and technicians who would build the gigantic dam and the turbines – thus Songo was born.

Today the village is still a busy settlement. Its entire population is employed by the HCB (**Hidroelétrica Cahora Bassa**) and visitors are only allowed entry if they present their passport at the control point.

Songo has a hotel, social club, filling station, post office, hospital, supermarket and paved airstrip. If you have made prior arrangements with HCB in Maputo, you can be taken on a fascinating guided tour of the power-generating plant and dam wall.

Fishing on Cahora Bassa ***

The fishing here is said to be reminiscent of the glory days of Lake Kariba (Zimbabwe) in the 1960s before it was overfished, but getting permission to camp and fish in the area may be a lengthy process. However, **Songo Fishing and Canoe Safaris**, a commercial company, is able to make the necessary arrangements.

Independent anglers should head for **Chicoa**. About 10km (6 miles) before Songo, turn left onto a potholed road signposted **Estima E Chicoa** and carry on for 40km (25 miles), through Chicoa to the lakeshore. Zimbabwean Piet Hougaard has a fishing camp near Mágoe.

TETE TOWN

Tete must rank as the hottest town in southern Africa. Midsummer temperatures on the blistering, bleached banks of the Zambezi sometimes edge towards 50°C (122°F)! As the town's only swimming pool, at the river's edge next to the bridge, is usually empty, there is little to recommend Tete as a stopover other than perhaps to refuel and buy some fresh bread. To be fair, Tete does have a reasonably comfortable but overpriced hotel, the **Zambeze**, as well as a fairly good riverside restaurant, while for the historically minded there are two interesting sandstone stockades, one located just upstream from the bridge and the other in town next to the military garrison.

Tete may never become one of Mozambique's most visited places, but its location on one of Africa's busiest transport routes lends it great strategic importance. Until 1992 travellers and truckers taking the short cut between Zimbabwe and Malawi via Tete were often shot at by bandits, even though this so-called Tete Corridor was protected by Zimbabwean soldiers. Today the road is in top condition – police with radar speed-traps are now the most serious hazard. Note that a negligible toll is payable on crossing the suspension bridge over the Zambezi into Tete, and that this is a favourite place to trap drivers who dare to exceed the 15kph (9½mph) speed restriction.

Above: *The bridge at Tete spans the Zambezi River.*
Opposite: *Roadside eateries, like this one on the road between Tete and Zóbuè, are a welcome sight.*

BEAUTIFUL BIRDS

The unique mixture of varying geological components, soils, relief, altitude and precipitation in the **Manica** and **Tete** provinces have produced a unique habitat that is rich in endemic fauna and flora. Here birds such as the **green-headed oriole** and the **moustache warbler** draw bird enthusiasts from all over the world.

From Beira to Tete, At a Glance

BEST TIMES TO VISIT

Avoid November to February, when it is so hot that an egg will cook beneath your hat. The driest period in **Beira** (50mm; 2in per month), and best time for malaria, is April to October. **Tete**'s climatic and malaria situation is much the same (without the cool sea breezes), but its monthly rainfall is only around half.

GETTING THERE

Beira and Tete are served by **LAM's domestic line**, with **international flights** between Johannesburg (South Africa) and Beira landing on Mondays. For information call Johannesburg, tel: (2711) 331-6082, fax: 331-7795, or Beira, tel: (3) 32-4141, fax: 32-8632. **Trains** between Beira and Machipanda on the Zimbabwe border run only on Tuesdays, Fridays and Saturdays (check with CFM-C, tel: (3) 32-1051, for the schedule). *Chapas* also link the towns in this area. Transportes Oliveiras **buses** run between Maputo and Beira on a daily basis. While Panthera Azul (*see* p. 42) has **luxury coaches** travelling from Johannesburg to Beira. An all-weather 4WD passenger vehicle service between Quelimane and Beira is offered by **Transportes Cocorico**, Pensão Moderna, Beira, tel: (3) 30-1174 during office hours, and tel: (3) 36-2198 after hours.

GETTING AROUND

City taxis (called 'tuksees') are usually fairly dilapidated. Wait for one at the airport or outside the more expensive hotels. Car hire firms represented in Beira are **Avis**, tel: (3) 30-1263, fax: 30-1265 and **Hertz**, tel: (3) 32-2315, fax: 32-2415. Never leave your car unattended in or around Beira as anything removable will be taken. *Chapas* are widely available, but only to places out of town.

WHERE TO STAY

Good accommodation is scarce, so book well in advance.

Beira
LUXURY
Hotel Embaixador, Rua Major Serpa Pinto, tel: (3) 32-3121/3, fax: 32-3788. Telephone in each room; air-conditioning; conference centre, and friendly staff.

Hotel Moçambique, Av. Daniel Napatima, tel: (3) 32-9351/6, fax: 32-5060. TV; air conditioning; shared telephones; swimming pool.

MID-RANGE
Hotel Residencial do Infante, 218 Rua Jaime Ferreira, tel: (3) 32-3042 Some rooms are air conditioned; good restaurant; noisy nightclub on weekends.

Hotel Miramar, Av. Matéus Sansão Muthemba, tel: (3) 32-2283. On the beachfront, lock-up parking; good food.

BUDGET
Bique's Beach Lodge and Camp site, Av. FPLM, Macúti suburb. Bique's booking office in Beira, tel: (3) 31-2853, fax: 32-7704. In Harare, Zimbabwe, tel: (2634) 74-5003, fax 74-4978. Right on the beach.

Clube Náutico, on Macúti beach, close to the hospital, tel: (3) 31-3093. Camping only; swimming pool; restaurant; clean ablutions (no running water); reasonable security.

Chimoio
MID-RANGE
Motel Moinho (The Mill), on the outskirts of town, tel: (51) 2-3130. Double rooms, suites, and a basic restaurant.

Manica
LUXURY COTTAGES
BUDGET CAMPING
Casa Msika Resort, Lake Chicamba, tel: (51) 2-2675, fax: 2-2701 in Chimoio; or Beira, tel: (3) 32-2796, fax: 32-4589. Rondavels equipped with bedding, towels and soap; swimming pool.

Tete
LUXURY
Hotel Zambeze, Av. Eduardo Mondlane, tel: (52) 2-3003. Good views; some rooms are air conditioned.

BUDGET
Pensão Alves, Av. 25 de Junho, tel: (52) 2-2523. Friendly service.

From Beira to Tete, At a Glance

WHERE TO EAT

Don't miss out on the delicious fresh produce at the municipal market, and small *quiosques*. Avoid meat and shellfish, unless eating at the better establishments.

Beira
Pic Nic,115 Rua Costa Serrão, tel: (3) 32 6518. Most popular and best restaurant in Beira; drinks rather expensive; booking is essential.

Restaurante Arcádia (Johnny's Place), Av. Poder Popular, tel: (3) 32-2266. A Beira favourite for 30 years.

Centro Hípico, On the Rua do Aeroporto, close to the junction with the EN6 (main road out of Beira), tel: (3) 302-030. Popular with the younger set.

Take-Away 2+1, 7 Rua 100, Maquinino (from Praça da India go up Av. 24 Julho and take the fourth left), tel: (3) 32-9883. A reputation for excellent Mozambican dishes.

O Zequinha (Clube Náutico da Beira), Av. FPLM, tel: 31-3093. Restaurant with a swimming pool; excellent food on a cool terrace overlooking the ocean.

Chimoio
Mauá, in the Feira Popular on the Chimoio bypass; no telephone. Favoured by the local business people.

Manica
Casa Msika, Chicamba Dam, tel: (51) 2-2675, fax: 2-2701 in Chimoio. Excellent, reasonably priced pub-restaurant.

Tete
Restaurante Freitas, on the river bank next to the bridge, tel: (52) 2-2709.

TOURS AND EXCURSIONS

Contact the **Sociedade de Safaris de Moçambique**, tel: (3) 32-3686 or 32-3152, to arrange a safari. There are **no formal city tour** operators, but hire a taxi, grab your guidebook and camera and let the driver show you around.
Gorongosa National Park is open for self-sufficient visitors.
Government ferries bound for Búzi leave the small boat harbour on Tuesday, Friday, Saturday and Sunday.
Enjoy fly-in **Cahora Bassa Fishing and Canoe Safaris** by contacting Vintage Air, Johannesburg, South Africa, tel/fax: (2711) 888-3168. Alternatively, drive via the town of Nyamapanda, on the border with Zimbabwe, and turn off to Songo before reaching Tete.

USEFUL CONTACTS

Beira
Beira Airport, tel: (3) 30-1071.
City Council, tel: (3) 32-2125 or 32-4123.
LAM, tel: (3) 32-4141, fax: 32-8632.
Tecnauto (vehicle repairs), tel: (3) 21-2893 or 21-2993.
Banco Commercial de Moçambique, tel: (3) 32-2173.
SabinAir Charter, tel: (3) 30-1392, fax: 30-1393.
Mariners' Relief Agency, tel: (3) 32-9071, fax: 31-1347 (Bonny Lynn). This company maintains the engines on the Zambezi ferry (Caia) and may be able to update you regarding Gorongosa National Park.
Railway Station (CFM), tel: (3) 32-1051 or 32-1033.

Tete
Hidrelétrica Cahora Bassa (HCB), tel: (52) 2-0059 or 2-2779.
Auto Reparadora de Tete, Av 25 Junho, tel: (52) 2-2581 or 2-3096.
For reliable and up-to-date information regarding both coastal and inland fishing in Mozambique contact Charles Norman, tel: (2711) 888-3168, Johannesburg, South Africa.

BEIRA	J	F	M	A	M	J	J	A	S	O	N	D
AVERAGE TEMP. °F	84	80	79	77	75	72	72	73	77	80	82	84
AVERAGE TEMP. °C	29	27	26	25	24	22	22	23	25	27	28	29
RAINFALL in	11	9	10	4	2	1.5	1.2	1	0.7	1.2	6	10
RAINFALL mm	280	220	260	100	60	40	30	25	20	30	145	260

7
North of the Zambezi

The wildly rugged and picturesque provinces of **Zambezia**, **Nampula**, **Cabo Delgado** and **Niassa** make up the area of Mozambique north of the raw and romantic **Zambezi River**. Within Mozambique the powerful currents of the Zambezi still form a formidable barrier both to movement between and development of the four northern provinces. This is mainly because there is no proper, accessible road bridge over the river downstream from Tete – the 3.7km (2½-mile) converted **rail bridge** between **Sena** and **Morrumbala** being served by extremely poor tracks on either side. While the vehicle and cargo **ferry** at **Caia** may have four powerful new engines and a capacity of 22 tonnes, access roads are often impassable from January to March. Thus the mighty Zambezi continues to divide Mozambique into two distinct regions: a south influenced by South Africa and Zimbabwe, and a north which relates to Malawi and Tanzania.

Until the late 19th century the northern Mozambique coast from **Chinde** to **Mocímboa da Praia** enjoyed most of the Portuguese government's attention. Apart from modest trading posts at Tete, Beira, Inhambane and Maputo Bay, the area south of the Zambezi was long considered too far away from maritime trading routes to warrant extensive development. This was the reason why former Lourenço Marques was declared the state capital only in 1898. During the previous four centuries Mozambique had functioned primarily as a trading and military post and **Mozambique Island** had been the principal city and busiest port.

DON'T MISS

*** Mozambique Island: fascinating, 400-year-old colonial history.
*** Zambezi delta: very impressive, especially when viewed from the air.
*** Seafood: the biggest and most succulent prawns available fresh from the sea.
** Nampula and Lichinga: stunning scenery on the drive between the two destinations.
** Praia da Wimbe: spend a week in a cosy bungalow.
* Ilhas das Querimbas: explore this remote and beautiful coral archipelago.

Opposite: *The entrance to the Fortaleza São Sebastião on Mozambique Island.*

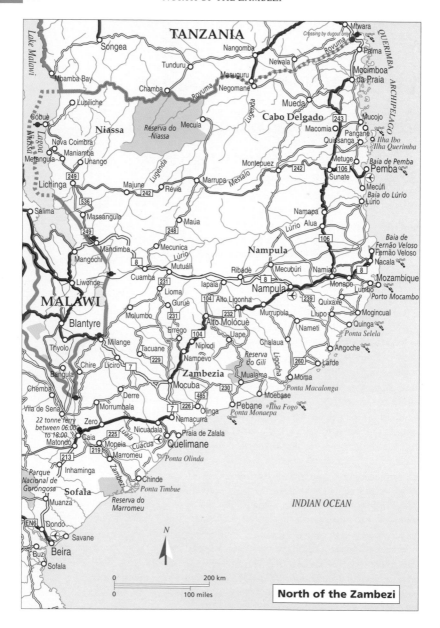

North of the Zambezi

Left: *Quelimane lies on the bank of the winding Rio dos Boas Sinais.*

QUELIMANE

Quelimane (pronounced 'Kelimani') is one of Africa's few good river ports. It lies on the **Rio dos Boas Sinais** (River of Good Omens), a name given to the mangrove-lined estuary by Vasco da Gama when he anchored there in 1498 on a mission to find a sea route to India. A *padrão* (stone pillar), erected at the river mouth to commemorate this landing, was claimed by the sea over 50 years ago. The river could also have been named Rio dos Sepulturas (River of Graves) as the first two Europeans to die in southern Africa were buried here, having succumbed to the combined ravages of scurvy and malaria.

Today over 100,000 people live in Quelimane, capital of Zambezia province, making it Mozambique's fourth-largest town. **Tea estates**, **coconut** and **cashew farms** on the coastal flats are the main providers of rural employment, while city dwellers manage to exist by trading, manufacturing and working in ventures that have survived decades of isolation. Most people live in the lively, colourful *bairros* that stretch out into the coconut plantations for some distance.

Main tribal groups are the Lómwè, Chuabo, Marende and Sena. Similar to the Tsonga and Shangaan of southern Mozambique (refugees from King Shaka's reign of terror a century ago), the Chuabo people clustered together deep in the fever-ridden mangrove swamps around Quelimane for protection against the Mwenu Mutapa.

Above: *Zalala Beach, once considered by Sir Malcolm Campbell for an attempt to break the land-speed record.* **Opposite:** *Beautiful, traditional Makua huts like this occur in Nampula province.*

Quelimane Harbour *

Quelimane is the terminus for the 96km (60-mile) railway from **Mocuba**, which is not in operation at present. From the station, a narrow-gauge line runs to the two concrete-and-steel jetties *(caias)* where steam engines once shunted goods to and from the harbour. Here the Rio dos Boas Sinais is 1.6km (1 mile) wide, and its nine-knot current, treacherous shifting sandbanks and 3.5m (11ft) tidal range make Quelimane harbour difficult to navigate. A century and a half ago, the British Royal Navy brigantine *Dart*, sent to pick up **David Livingstone**, sank on the sandbar lying across the river mouth, resulting in the loss of eight crew members. Today the river is constantly dredged to provide passage for the coasters seeking cargo of copra, fish and rice. A new berth for fishing trawlers, as well as refrigeration facilities, have recently been completed 2km (1¼ miles) from Quelimane.

Zalala Beach **

At the end of a tarmac road north from Quelimane, that runs through an endless forest of coconut trees, you will discover Zalala beach and enormous succulent **prawns**. Dragged in by the local fishermen, **barracuda** (*Sphyraene barracuda*), squid or **bluefin kingfish** (*Caranx melampygus*) may also appear in the nets. Praia de Zalala lies white and flat and because it is so isolated resembles a lost runway for some forgotten aircraft. The beach is long and hard-packed enough to have been considered for one of Sir Malcolm Campbell's attempts at breaking the world land-speed record. Should you own a **land yacht**, bring it to Zalala and sail off into the sunset.

Zalala town consists of a small group of holiday houses and a basic restaurant with a bar and dance floor, and is flanked by little fishing villages.

The Zambezi Delta

This delta, a remote unspoiled wilderness of shifting sand islands, savannah and mangrove trees, is one of the few places in Mozambique where big game (elephant, buffalo, rhino and roan antelope) is still present. **Chinde**, a small port on the deepest tributary, was once busy with cranes loading thousands of tonnes of sugar into cargo ships. Successive cyclones have almost obliterated the site of old Chinde and a new town was built further inland. A light rail system once linked Chinde to the now derelict Sena sugar estates further upriver on the banks of the Zambezi.

The best way to view the 1500km² (579 sq mile) expanse of channels and islands is from the air. Three **air charter** companies are based in Quelimane and it is fairly inexpensive to hire a light plane for a low-level flyover of the delta. TTA in particular have, in the past, been reliable and reasonably priced. You can fly in, land at Chinde and spend a few days exploring the railways before you are picked up again (by prior arrangement), or enjoy an **aerial wildlife-spotting safari** over the unique delta habitat – by far the cheaper option.

Nampula

In 1967 the Portuguese, in the face of Frelimo's growing disenchantment with **colonial rule**, decided to establish Nampula as their main military base. Its location on the important **Nacala–Malawi railway** and on the north–south overland route contributed to attach to Nampula the label: 'capital of the north'.

Despite its relative isolation the town is an important service centre for the surrounding area and provides many essential amenities. Diesel and petrol are usually available, but the latter can become quite difficult to obtain during seasonal periods of bad weather, when the road tanker gets bogged down on the muddy roads.

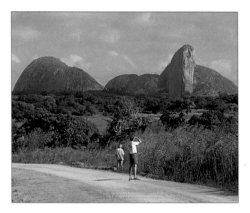

Nampula is useful for travellers, because **visas** can be extended here. The **airport** is served by LAM, linking the town to Beira and Maputo. There is a hospital, varied accommodation, public telephones, some good restaurants, and a well-stocked **municipal market**. The **Clube CVFM** (Railway Club) is even able to offer a swimming pool with clean water, though they do tend to charge the earth for the privilege of using it.

Above: *A rock climber's paradise – the granite outcrops in Nampula province.*
Opposite: *The entrance to the port captain's villa on Mozambique Island.*

WHERE THERE IS NO BRIDGE

In the 1970s, the **Portuguese** engaged in major road-building programmes to facilitate swift troop movement. The paving of the road from Beira, across the Zambezi to Quelimane, Nampula and Pemba, clearly a strategically important route, was a major priority. In 1975, work stopped due to the **sudden withdrawal** by the new Portuguese government – many large bridges had not yet been built. The badly rutted detours, leading off the road from **Mocuba to Alto Molócuè** to the old steel-and-pole bridges, are a living monument to the bizarre occurrences of 1975.

The Quelimane–Nampula Road **

As far as **Nicuadala**, where you turn right, the road surface is damaged. Until **Mocuba**, a tidy little outpost without a fuel station, the road is either tarmac or graded gravel and should be passable, except during the odd cyclone. Here you'll find one of Mozambique's latest signposts pointing to various mysterious places, none of which is **Alto Molócuè**, your next objective. Despite being virtually cut off in the wet season, it is a surprisingly busy village.

The 188km (117 miles) of EN104 between Mocuba and Alto Molócuè appear fairly benign at first, but watch out! A little after the turnoff to **Errego**, some 85km (53 miles) out of Mocuba, the smooth tarmac road reaches a river without a bridge. If you're driving at night, you may discover this anomaly by ending nosefirst in mud! To avoid any disasters on this route, keep looking well ahead: bush flattened by vehicles making a detour down to the old bridge is always an indication of trouble ahead.

Between Mocuba and Quelimane lies a wonderful pristine stretch of **miombo forests**, **clear streams** and prolific **birdlife** on this, one of Africa's most remote and fascinating overland routes. However, the realities and implications of travelling on roads which disappear unexpectedly in a region where fuel, spares and repair services are unknown and heavy rain can leave you stranded between flooding rivers, should not be underestimated!

MOZAMBIQUE ISLAND

Mozambique Island is located where the Mozambique Channel is at its narrowest and Madagascar is only 350km (217 miles) to the east – one of the reasons why first the Arabs and later the Portuguese turned the island into a major **fortified port city**. Other features which favoured over a thousand years of foreign occupation are **safe anchorage** and fortunate location in relation to the monsoonal trade winds.

Though the **Arabs** probably began trading with East Africa around AD500, the formal documentation of their 1500-year dominance in this sector of the Indian Ocean was not a Portuguese priority. What is certain is that sultans held sway in this area when Portuguese explorer **Vasco da Gama** steered his 150-tonne caravel into the calm waters off the island during 1498.

This tiny isle, 2500m (8202ft) long and 600m (1969ft) at its widest point, is a **microcosm** of the major tribal, cultural, historical and linguistic influences which have formed modern Mozambique. The island has been dubbed Africa's 'meeting point of civilizations'. Persians, Indians and Arabs came to trade and stayed; the Portuguese settled for 500 years; the Dutch and the English tried, in vain, to dislodge them; and today African people still stop over here during fishing expeditions.

Early commerce centred on cloth, beads and spices from the East which were bartered for **ivory, gold, precious stones** and **slaves** from the African hinterland. Eager to

'MISSANGA' ARAB BEADS

The currency of trade during Arab times were **porcelain trading beads**. Belligerent newcomers to the island, the Portuguese sank many Arab vessels close to Mozambique Island during the **trade war** between 1498 and 1504. Nearly 500 years later the beads are still washing ashore. Along with modern plastic and glass baubles, *missanga* are threaded onto fishing line making colourful necklaces which are sold to visitors.

MOZAMBIQUE'S NATIONAL MUSEUM

Situated on the bottom end of Mozambique Island's Av. Eduardo Mondlane, next to a cinema, the **Museu Nacional de Moçambique** is housed in a marble neo-classical building which was once the governor's palace. Artefacts from all over the country provide a fascinating insight into the country, both past and present. Behind the museum is a Makonde co-operative where carvers sit and get on with their trade, while their children bash out tunes on marimbas.

ISLAND MOISTURIZER

The beaming, white-smeared face of a Makua woman could well be Mozambique Island's symbol. Wood from the **nciro tree** is ground into a fine powder, mixed with water to form a paste and then packed onto the face to keep the skin soft and to prevent sun damage. The masque is removed at night, when the menfolk return from fishing or boat building.

share in (and dominate) the ancient trade routes, King Emanuel of Portugal sent out scouts to blaze a trail to India. Nine years after Vasco da Gama clashed with Arab sultans on the island, the Portuguese formally occupied it, building a small **stockade** and leaving behind a mere 15 men to protect this outpost.

Fortaleza São Sebastião ★★★

In 1558, using granite quoins shipped as ballast from Portugal on the light caravels, construction on the fortress of St Sebastian began. Due to the lengthy voyage to and from the motherland, the 12m-high (39ft), 750m-long (2460ft) walls of the fortress were completed only 40 years later. For years São Sebastião was Africa's largest structure south of the Sahara, meant to symbolize the impregnable foothold of the Portuguese in Africa. However, it took the economic realities of the 20th century, not foreign invaders, to finally dislodge the settlers. Bigger modern ships needed deeper ports, and isolation, long an asset, now became an impediment. By 1960, the island had lost all of its former importance to the Portuguese and was left to rot.

500-YEAR-OLD WATER

Fortaleza São Sebastião was ingeniously designed to catch rainfall and channel the precious water into a huge cistern dug into the central courtyard. This reservoir enabled the Portuguese soldiers to withstand long sieges by the Dutch, who had to collect water from the mainland where locals were hostile to intrusions. Recently a Swiss aid organization completed a project which pipes water onto the island. Still today, gaily dressed women queue daily around the fortress cistern, and leave with buckets of water on their heads.

Capela de Nossa Senhora do Baluarte ★★

This church, which lies in ruins behind the fortress on the northeastern point of the island, was built in 1503. Although brutally vandalized and severely dilapidated, if you look inside you will see a crumbling memorial tablet.

Palácio de São Paulo ★★★

Originally constructed in 1619 to house the island's governor and administration, St Paul's Palace is now a **museum** and has been declared a **World Heritage Site**. Unfortunately the enormous funding required to turn around some 50 years of neglect has not been forthcoming. The curator, Pedro, is doing his best to protect the beautifully carved **Goanese** furniture, the **Portuguese** oil paintings, the fragile **Chinese** pottery and porcelain, and the **Indian** tapestries and **Arab** drapes from damage by a badly leaking roof. It is open 09.00–17:00 Wednesday to Friday, 09:00–15:00 at weekends; closed on Monday and Tuesday.

Chocas-Mar ★★

On an empty beach looking out onto **Baia da Condúcia**, once a resort for affluent Nampula residents, some of the holiday homes at Chocas-Mar have been renovated. The road is in fairly shocking condition and when you get to **Mossuril**, you will need to ask for directions to get there. Apart from the fine, curving beach at Chocas, **Mossuril Bay** is favoured by mating **southern right whales** from July to October each year, a tender spectacle well worth the journey. Since it is not possible to book accommodation, it is best to arrive during the week – the weekends are popular with people from Nampula and Nacala.

With a population of about 14,000, the village section of Mozambique Island is one of the most densely populated places in Africa. There are no ablution facilities, so the beaches are used as public toilets. If you're keen to suntan, take a dip or snorkel, rather catch a dhow to the nearby Goa or Snake (*Das Cobras*) islands where the sand and the sea are clean.

Opposite: *The 16th-century Capela de Nossa Senhora do Baluarte overlooks the sea.*
Below: *This bandstand graces the square in front of the Palácio de São Paulo.*

PEMBA

Before 1975, Pemba, the capital of Cabo Delgado province, was called **Porto Amelia**. The residents have dubbed it Mozambique's **papaya paradise**, which is fairly apt, as this little port is located on a headland squeezed between a magnificent inland bay and an idyllic beach where tall papaya trees lend their shade.

Although most visitors fly into Pemba on LAM, the 526km (326-mile) stretch of road between Nampula and Pemba, despite being severely potholed in places, is passable in a standard car.

Seen from the bay, the white, flat-roofed buildings of Pemba's old town are typical of many of Africa's original colonial towns. Built on a hill, the town climbs steeply from the quayside to the Art Deco cinema at the top of the hill. Pedestrians are well looked after by flights of marble steps which allow shortcuts across the corners of the 'switch-back' roads. These begin next to the municipal market and climb steeply, crossing half a dozen streets, before ending near the **Migração** building where your visa can be extended if necessary.

Opposite: *Boardgames are the speciality of this little workshop in Pemba.*
Below: *The idyllic sand and sea of Pemba's popular beach, Praia da Wimbe.*

Pemba's scenic **promenade** runs parallel to the mouth of the bay, before swinging right onto the main avenue to the airport and out of town. At a traffic circle overlooked by the **Banco Comercial de Moçambique** and the **Hotel Cabo Delgado**, a turn up the hill will take you on to **Avenida Eduardo Mondlane**, the main thoroughfare through Pemba's newer, more modern uptown quarter *(cima)*. Also on Eduardo Mondlane, you will come across an art gallery, two supermarkets, **Viatur Travel Agency** (which offers excursions, accommodation and car hire), a video rental, a hairdresser and a dress shop. The **governor's residence** is on the left near the top of this avenue, from where you can enjoy a panoramic view of the bay.

> **PEMBA BAY**
>
> South of the Tanzanian border, Pemba is reputed to be the world's largest inland bay. Its entrance is only 2km (1½ miles) wide, opening up to a beautiful blue expanse of water with an area of around 375km² (144 sq miles) and a uniform depth of about 24m (79ft). It is rumoured that the German U-boats (submarines) of World War II were provided with supplies here by sympathizers.

Traditional Markets ★★★

Surrounding Pemba (and most other large towns in Mozambique) are the *bairros*, which were referred to as 'native quarters' in the colonial days. Pemba's most colourful *bairro*, Paquite Quete (pronounced 'pakiti-ket'), is tucked in under coconut palms in a former mangrove swamp between the bay mouth and the docks. Here, in an area the size of three or four football fields, fishermen, boat-builders, basket weavers, carpenters, traders, mechanics, smugglers, jewellers, mothers and children go about their daily business. There are *quiosques* and mosques, schools and traditional healers, but it is at the *bazares* (traditional markets) where you'll find Mozambique's lively soul on display (at a negotiable price).

Only 20 or 30 minutes' walk away, other *bazares* worth investigating are in *bairros* **Natite** (just off Av. Eduardo Mondlane), **Ingonane** and **Cariaco** (on the way to Wimbe beach, before Heroes' Square), and **Wimbe**, which is inland from **Praia da Wimbe**. Trust a local to show you around and you will venture where few foreigners have been before. Enquire about the *esculturos* (sculptors) at the **Cooperativo Makonde**, situated on Wimbe beach route a short distance from the Praça dos Heróis.

Above: *This picture-perfect little villa is on Ibo Island.*
Below: *A silversmith at work in Ibo Island's fort.*
Opposite: *The old Fortaleza de São João Baptista is but a ruined shadow of its former self.*

Around Pemba

Pack a picnic lunch and head for glorious **Chuiba beach**, past Wimbe beach. The solitude and clear water make up for the lack of facilities. The inhabitants of the fishing village nearby are friendly, but petty theft is rife.

Hire a 4WD vehicle from Viatur and tour around the bay, through coastal forests, to **Metuge** village, and **Pangane** beach 125km (78 miles) further. You can motor out to quaint **Mecúfi** fishing hamlet, 35km (22 miles) south of Pemba, or charter the catamaran which is owned by Pero and anchored near the Pemba docks.

Ibo Island ★★★

Ibo is just one of over 30 coral islands that form the **Arquipélago das Querimbas**, stretching for 250km (156 miles) from Ilha Mefunvo in the south to Ilha Tecomaji in the north. Mentioned in eighth-century Arab writings, the

Portuguese only arrived some 700 years later. The Arabs had chosen the island for settlement because it was easy to defend against the 'sackers' from Madagascar. Initially one of the country's most affluent populations, Ibo's settlement was elevated to the status of town in 1761.

Fortifications on Ibo had commenced in 1754. The erection of the **Fort of São João Baptista** began 17 years later, and apparently took only a year to complete. Details of its construction are registered on two plaques, one above the fortified door, the other inside the entrance tunnel.

Originally a centre for Arab traders and much later the flourishing capital of northern Mozambique, Ibo Island's formerly impressive mansions and magnificent villas now lie roofless and in ruins. These crumbling houses, imitations of the gracious homes of 17th- and 18th-century Portugal, echo with the ghosts of officials who enjoyed the opulent lifestyle of the old administrative seat and commercial centre of northern Mozambique.

Querimba Island *

The Gessners, a family of German extraction, own coconut plantations on Querimba Island as well as a delightful home. They also have a guest cottage which they let out to their rare visitors.

At low tide, it is possible to walk with a guide through the magnificent tangled mangrove forest that separates Ibo and Querimba.

Mocímboa da Praia *

A small, steamy fishing port with a post office, customs post and *pensão*, Mocímboa da Praia is the closest large town to Mozambique's border with **Tanzania**. The setting on a small bay, complete with tiny island and coconut-tree-lined beach is certainly postcard pretty. The sheltered position has a severe drawback though – sea breezes can't moderate the tropical heat and humidity, making the town an uncomfortable place to be in, even during June and July.

Mueda *

It was at Mueda that a momentous event occurred during 1964, setting in motion formal resistance to Portuguese rule. Makonde elders, rebelling against the confiscation of their land by the settlers, attended a meeting with the Portuguese governor here and hundreds of them were machine-gunned down during an ensuing riot. Today the town has a memorial to the Mueda Massacre and remains the administrative centre for the Makonde people.

> ### FORTALEZA DE SÃO JOÃO BAPTISTA
>
> This pentagonal fort, typical of the 18th century, had space for 300 troops, food storage and armouries. The entire population of **Ibo** and nearby **Quelimane** and **Matemo** sought refuge here during Arab, French, British and Dutch forays. From 1960–74 activists resisting Portuguese colonial rule were kept here as political prisoners. The fort is now a historical monument.

North of the Zambezi At a Glance

BEST TIMES TO VISIT

Tropical cyclones hit the **coast-line**, on average, once every five years during the humid November to March period. The rest of the year is **hot**, with May to October the **driest** months. The climate around Lichinga is modified by altitude: summers are warm, but in winter it can become quite cold at night.

GETTING THERE

This region is one of the most **isolated** in Africa and can be completely cut off during the rains (December–April). If using your own vehicle, prepare and plan accordingly. Quelimane, Nampula, Pemba and Lichinga are served by **LAM**, but flights are **often fully booked**. Be sure to contact LAM well in advance. Quelimane, tel: (4) 21-2800; Nampula, tel: (6) 21-3311; Pemba, tel: (72) 3251; Lichinga, tel: (71) 2434. On Mondays and Thursdays **Malawi Railways** trains travel from Liwonde (Malawi) to Cuamba (Mozambique) from where there is a passenger service once a day to Nampula. Assuming that the ferry over the Zambezi at Caia is operating, **Transportes Cocorico** run a 4WD passenger vehicle service between Quelimane and Beira. Contact Senhor Brandão at Pensão Moderna, Beira, tel: (3) 30-1174 during office hours and tel: (3) 36-2198 after hours.

GETTING AROUND

Chapas and buses operate from Nampula to Nacala, Mozambique Island, Pemba and Mocímboa da Praia, Palma and Mueda. Other towns are served by irregular, uncomfort-able transport trucks, suitable for the adventurous only. **Zalala Beach** can be reached via *chapa* on a 35km (21 mile) dead-end tarmac road.

WHERE TO STAY

Quelimane
MID-RANGE
Pensão Ideal, Av. Filipe S Magaia, tel: (4) 21-2739. Well-run; excellent food.

Zalala Beach
MID-RANGE
Complexo Kass-Kass, at the end of the tar road take the sand track to the right. No telephone. Beach houses; bring along all you will need.

Alto Molócuè
BUDGET
Pensão Fambauoi, off the praça; no telephone. Friendly staff; quaint outside kitchen.

Gúruè
MID-RANGE
Pousada Monte Neve, Av. Eduardo Mondlane, tel: (6) 21. Magnificent views.

Nampula
LUXURY
Hotel Tropical, tel: (6) 21-2232. Not cheap, but good value for your money.

MID-RANGE
Hotel Nampula, Av. 1 de Maio, tel: (6) 21-2147. Good accommodation; friendly staff.

MID-RANGE
Angoche
Pensão Oceânia, centrally located, tel: (6) 72343. Time-less ambience in the heart of this historic trading centre.

Mossuril
BUDGET
Chocas Mar Cottages, 26km (16 miles) from Monapo turn left to Mossuril on the road to Mozambique Island. No telephone. The setting alone, is worth the relatively high rental demanded by the caretaker.

Mozambique Island
BUDGET
Pousada de Moçambique, in the museum area *(bairro da museu)* of the island, tel: (6) 5-8134. A shabby two-storey hotel with 20 rooms, bucket showers, erratic electricity. The walls may be mildewed, the beds collapsing and the plumbing out of order, but camping is not a great alter-native, due to petty theft.

Nacala
BUDGET
Hotel Nacala, lower city, tel: (6) 526-6350. Basic amenities.

Pemba
MID-range
Complexo Nautilus, Wimbe Beach, tel: (72) 3520.

North of the Zambezi At a Glance

Six- and four-bed chalets right on the beach. Superb views and snorkelling.

Hotel Cabo Delgado, 28 Av. Eduardo Mondlane, tel: (72) 2559. Clean and comfortable.

BUDGET
Pensão Baia, Av. I de Maio, tel: (72) 3435. Basic but clean.

Cuamba
BUDGET
Pensão S Miguel, on the main road, tel: (71) 59. Rooms with en-suite bathroom; restaurant and off-street parking.

Lichinga
MID-RANGE
Pousada de Lichinga, corner Av. Samora Machel and Filipe S Magaia, tel: (71) 2648. Best of a poor choice.

WHERE TO EAT

Quelimane
Pensão Ideal, (see Where to Stay). The best food in town.

Zalala Beach
Complexo Kass-Kass, (see Where to Stay). Secluded outside bar; catch of the day served at tables under thatched umbrellas.

Nampula
Clube de CVFM, Rua 3 de Fevereiro, one block in front of the Hotel Lurio, near the railway station, tel: (6) 21-2979. Clean, air-conditioned, medium priced.

Mozambique Island
Pousada de Moçambique, (see Where to Stay). If your group is larger than two people be sure to order half a day in advance, as supplies come from the mainland.

Pemba
Restaurant Cabo Delgado, Av. Eduardo Mondlane, tel: (72) 3552. Serves the best food in Pemba.

Pensão Baia, (see Where to Stay). Good value for money.

Lichinga
Pousada Lichinga, (see Where to Stay). This eatery is not used to feeding foreigners, but it does try.

SHOPPING

A range of beautiful carvings and crafts is available from the traditional markets.

TOURS AND EXCURSIONS

For **air flips** or **road safaris** from Pemba, on which you will be able to spot elephants, buffalos, crocodiles, hippos and other game along the Rovuma River, contact **Viatur Travel Agency** (Luis Feria), tel: (72) 3431, fax: 2249, telex: 6775 VIATU.

Why not enjoy a **boat trip** from Pemba to the beautiful Querimba Archipelago? Boats may be hired from the **Complexo Nautilus**, alternatively arrange for a dhow or motor launch from the *bairro* Paquete-Quete.

USEFUL CONTACTS

In the case of medical emergencies contact the **Red Cross Ambulance** (*Cruz Vermelha*):
Lichinga, tel: (71) 2548;
Quelimane, tel: (4) 21-2200;
Nampula, tel: (6) 21-3693.
In Pemba, contact the hospital, tel: (72) 2211.
For **meteorological information:**
Pemba, tel: (72) 2435;
Nampula, tel: (6) 21-4076;
Lichinga, tel: (71) 2454;
Quelimane, tel: (4) 21-2800.
Police: Pemba, tel: (72) 2652; Nampula tel: (6) 199;
Lichinga, tel: (71) 2828;
Quelimane, tel: (4) 199 or 21-3131.
Ports: Pemba, tel: (72) 2720 and Nacala, tel: (6) 52-6637.
For **scuba diving** at the Querimba islands north of Pemba, get in touch with **Rosanna (Pvt) Ltd**, Harare, Zimbabwe, tel/fax: (2634) 86-0152.

NAMPULA	J	F	M	A	M	J	J	A	S	O	N	D
AVERAGE TEMP. °F	79	77	79	75	73	72	72	73	77	80	82	80
AVERAGE TEMP. °C	26	25	26	24	23	22	22	23	25	27	28	27
RAINFALL in	10	9.8	7.5	4	1	0.7	0.7	0.5	1	1.2	1.5	5.5
RAINFALL mm	260	250	190	100	25	20	20	15	25	30	40	140

Travel Tips

Tourist Information

Mozambique has **diplomatic missions** in France, Germany, Italy, Portugal, the Russian Federation, the UK, Sweden, Switzerland and the USA.
Public Information Bureau (BIP), 772 Av. Francisco Orlando Magumbwe, Maputo, tel: (1) 49-0200, fax: 49-2622, e-mail: GEO2 BIP-MOZ. Though not a formal tourist-oriented operation, BIP has a video room and reference library and sells books, magazines and maps.
The **Mozambique National Tourist Company** (Empresa Nacional de Turismo), Maputo, tel: (1) 42-1794, fax: 42-1795, and Johannesburg, South Africa, tel: (2711) 339-7275, is Mozambique's official tourist office. ENT also act as brokers for various destinations and tour operators in Mozambique.

Entry Requirements

All visitors need a **passport** (valid for at least six months after departure) and a **visa**. Visas are rarely issued on arrival. At Maputo, Inhambane, Beira, Quelimane and Pemba, yachties will be allowed ashore to apply for a visa which can

be issued within 36 hours (multiple-entry visas essential if more stops along the Mozambican coast are anticipated). Visitors arriving by vehicle must have a valid **driver's licence** and the car's original **registration papers**. A temporary import permit and MVA (third-party) insurance (bought at the border) will be demanded at checkpoints throughout the country. It is a good idea to carry certified copies of your driver's licence as the police are sometimes reluctant to hand back original documents without first extracting a 'fine'.

Customs

Declare your money on the **arrival form** (the form must be handed in on departure).
Electronic equipment must be declared. Other goods may attract import duties if the official decides you intend to sell them in Mozambique.
Pets may be brought in from South Africa and Zimbabwe only if you have a vet's certificate indicating that they have had all their inoculations. You may have some difficulty bringing them back home.

Health Requirements

The tropical climate is ideal for *anopheles* mosquitoes which transmit **malaria**. (Consult your physician before travelling into Mozambique.) **Bilharzia** in rivers and lakes and **AIDS** also pose serious threats for the foolhardy. Tap water is not potable, but many lodges and hotels have their own safe borehole water. Drink plenty of liquids as humidity reduces the body's ability to cool itself and be sure to protect yourself from the strong sun. Visitors from, or passing through, a **yellow fever** zone require a valid **International Certificate of Vaccination**. Cholera and smallpox vaccinations are not required nor is there any form of AIDS screening for visitors.

Getting There

By air: Maputo International Airport is served by carriers from Europe (Paris and Lisbon), South Africa and Zimbabwe. **Beira Airport** receives one LAM flight from Johannesburg per week. The status of **Vilankulo Airport** has been upgraded to that of 'airport of entry'.

By road: Good tarmac roads lead from South Africa, Swaziland, Zimbabwe and western Malawi. The absence of bridges over the Rovuma River blocks access from Tanzania. Luxury buses operate from Durban and Johannesburg (both in South Africa) to Maputo and Beira. Contact tel: (2711) 337-7409.

By rail: There are regular trains three times weekly between Maputo and Johannesburg , tel: (2711) 820-2479. The line from Mutare (Zimbabwe) to Beira is served irregularly; call CFM, Maputo, tel: (1) 43-0020. Twice a week trains run from Liwonde to Nayuchi (Malawi), from where there are daily trains to Nampula. Contact Morton Thyolani in Blantyre, Malawi, tel: (09265) 64-0844.

By boat: No scheduled passenger service to Mozambique exists at present. **Starlight Cruises**, Johannesburg, tel: (2711) 884-7680, do include Inhaca and Bazaruto islands in their package tours.

What to Pack

A sunhat is essential, as are long shirts and trousers to ward off mosquitoes in the evenings. Beachwear may be daring if you wish, but women should cover their legs with a sarong and men should don shirt and shorts off the beach. A warm jacket and trousers for winter evenings, an umbrella for the sudden tropical downpours and smart-casual evening wear for some restaurants and clubs may be needed.

Money Matters

Currency: Unit of currency is the **metical** (MT), plural meticais. A quanto (1000 meticais) is also referred to as um mil. Notes come in denominations of 100 and 200 (rare); 500; 1000; 5000; 10,000; 20,000 and 50,000. Ask for some cash in smaller denominations when changing money as stall holders in markets and along the road don't carry much change. Coins exist but are unpopular.

Exchange: Money can be exchanged at banks, hotels (poor rate) and Mercados Secundário de Câmbios (Bureaux de Change) where you'll get best rates for US$ and SA Rand. Banco Standard Totta and Banco de Moçambique (open 08:15–11:00 Monday to Friday, closed on Saturdays and Sundays) hold the exchange monopoly. Only the most upmarket hotels and restaurants in Maputo accept **credit cards**. The Banco Comercial de Mozambique (Maputo) will give the equivalent of R500 (US$100) per day in meticais against your credit card.

Traveller's cheques are converted at banks, at secondary exchange markets and at more expensive hotels. Banks may charge commission per cheque, regardless of denomination.

Tipping: Waiters and other workers appreciate tips.

Accommodation

Due to a decline in standards (except at **hotels** Polana and Cardoso in Maputo), the one-to-five-star grading system has become meaningless.

Good morning • *Bom dia*
Good evening • *Boa noite*
How are you? • *Como está?*
May I? • *Da licença?*
Please • *Por favor*
Yes • *Sim*
No • *Não*
Fine • *Tudo bem*
No problem • *Não faz mal*
Get me a taxi •
Chamar um taxi
I have a reservation •
Eu fiz uma reserva
Have you got . . .? • *Tem . . .?*
I would like that thing
(pointing to it) •
Gostaria d'esta coisa
How much? • *Quanto custa?*
I am lost • *Eu estou perdido*
Where is the doctor? •
Onde está um médico?

Outside of Maputo there are no five-star quality hotels, but comfortable **lodges** (from self-catering to full board) dot the coastline from Ponta Malongane and the Incomáti River Camp in the south to the *campismos* at Maxixe and Morrungulo a little further up the coast, and the Complexo Náutilus near Pemba.

The small, quaint **boarding houses** (*pensões*) range from the 'rather-sleep-in-your-car' variety to delightfully homely places where you can rest and recuperate. Running water is rare, but friendly service and clean sheets are the norm. Reasonably good and affordable accommodation cannot meet the demands and it is recommended that visitors book at least six months in advance to be assured of a reservation.

Eating Out

The predominance and variety of seafood reflects Mozambique's maritime location. Restaurants range from pricey-international (US$100 per plate) to simple-sidewalk (US$1 per plate). Many establishments specialize in spicy Indo–Portuguese cuisine such as curries and barbecued prawns, while market stalls may offer simple local fare like *mu-khuwane* (spinach and shrimps). The variety of fresh produce on sale at the markets increases towards the north, while prices tend to increase towards the south.

Transport

Air: The capital cities of eight of Mozambique's 10 provinces (Inhambane and Xai-Xai excluded), are served by the domestic wing of LAM (Linhas Aéreas de Mozambique). Demand for seats usually far outstrips supply, so booking at least six months in advance is recommended. Various well-established air charter companies provide services out of Maputo, Beira, Quelimane, Nampula and Pemba.
Road: The principal coastal road (Estrada Nacional 1, or **EN1**) which links Maputo, Xai-Xai, Inhambane, Vilankulo and Beira, has been upgraded. All roads linking Mozambique to its neighbouring countries have either been repaired or are presently receiving attention. In the Zambezia, Nampula, Cabo Delgado and Niassa provinces 4WD vehicles are essential during the rainy season (December–April).

Road rules: Although to the newcomer traffic will appear anarchic, *Mozambicanos* (should) drive on the left. Speed limits within any built-up area is 30kph (18½ mph), including along sections of rural roads which simply pass a trading store. Outside urban areas, the general speed limit is 100kph (62 mph). Specified short stretches of road (i.e. the bridge over the Zambezi at Tete) have speed limits of 15kph (9mph). Mozambique's traffic police may not have helicopters and fast cars, but they do have radar speed-trapping devices, so beware!
Car hire: Avis and **Hertz** are represented in Maputo and Beira. Unless you are doing a round trip from these two cities, you may have great difficulty hiring a vehicle. In Pemba, **Viatur** sometimes has vehicles available for hire. Overland visitors driving their own vehicle are required to purchase **third-party insurance** (*seguro*) at the border. Visitors are advised to carry a fully comprehensive travel insurance and a **medical evacuation policy**, which can be issued by such organizations as Euro-assist or Med-rescue International.
Petrol is widely available south of the Zambezi, costs a little more than in South Africa and is much more expensive than in Zimbabwe. **Diesel** is 40% cheaper than petrol.
Buses: Coach services offering varying comfort and reliability link Maputo to Beira, stopping at all large towns in between. Try **Transportes Virginias**,

SIGNS	
Direito •	Right
Esquerda •	Left
Paragem •	Bus stop
Desvio •	Detour
Controle •	Check-point
Entrada proibida •	No entry
Paragem proibida •	No stopping
Rotatória •	Traffic circle
Cidade •	City/town
Sem saida •	Cul-de-sac
Fechado •	Closed
Covas •	Potholes
Perigo •	Danger
Posto Sanitário •	Health post
Passagem •	Level crossing
Entrada •	Entrance
Saida •	Exit
PPM •	Police station
Obras •	Road works
Avenida •	Avenue
Rua •	Street
Praia •	Beach

tel: (1) 42-2225 or 42-7003, or **Transportes Oliveiras**, tel: (1) 42-1634 (both in Maputo). **Trains:** There is a daily passenger service from Maputo to Ressano Garcia and from Nampula to Cuamba.

Business Hours

Normal working hours for shops and offices are 07:30–12:30 and 14:00–17:30 Monday to Friday, and 09:00–13:30 and 15:00–18:30 on Saturday. Sidewalk *quiosques* stay open late into the night in Maputo and Beira. Some bars and nightclubs are open through the night on Fridays and Saturdays.

Time Difference

Mozambique is two hours ahead of Greenwich Mean (or Universal Standard) Time, one hour ahead of European Winter Time, and seven hours ahead of the USA's Eastern Standard Winter Time. Sydney is eight hours ahead of Mozambique. Mozambique Island is far enough east for the sun to rise an hour earlier than in Zimbabwe or South Africa, nevertheless these countries share a common time zone with Mozambique.

Communications

Major towns have a satellite telephone system, but getting through can be difficult. Local calls can be made from any *Telefone Pública*, international calls and faxes from expensive hotels and *Telecomuniçoes*, usually close to the post offices (*correios*). **Dialling codes** are: Maputo 1; Xai-Xai 22; Beira 3; Inhambane 23; Quelimane 4; Tete and Songo 52; Nampula and Nacala 6; and Pemba 72. Mozambique has two phone directories: *Zona Zul* (Maputo, Gaza and Inhambane province); *Zona Centro Norte* for the rest. Post offices are open 07:30–12:30 and 14:30–16:30 Monday to Friday, but are closed over weekends.

Electricity

Power supplied is 220 volts AC, but as variations are common, appliances should be surge-protected. Bring along a universal adapter plug.

Weights and Measures

The metric system was introduced in the early 1960s. A pocket fisherman's spring balance is a very useful item, as market scales are notoriously inaccurate.

Health Precautions

The **tropical climate** carries with it a high incidence of insect as well as water-borne diseases and infection. Most family doctors in developed countries have never treated **malaria** cases. Consult organizations dealing with tropical diseases for advice, bearing in mind that new strains of malaria, resistant to both chloroquine and pyrimethamine, occur throughout Mozambique. Enquire about the possible side effects of the newer more effective prophylactics and treatments such as Larium and Halofantrine.

Tap **water** is not safe to drink unless the source is an uncontaminated borehole at one of the lodges. Boil all your water or be sure to drink only the bottled variety which is widely available. It is safest to assume that all lakes and rivers are infested with **bilharzia**. Use **sun lotions** with the highest protection factor. Try one out before your holiday to see whether your skin tolerates it. A tan may be what you came for, but is it worth the risk of skin cancer? The longer it takes for your skin to change to that beautiful brown, the longer it will stay that way. **AIDS** is rife in Mozambique and the usual precautions applicable elsewhere should be followed. Since blood at the hospitals may not have been screened for the HIV virus, opt for the evacuation option if you need a blood transfusion and are in doubt. Stonefish, bluebottles, hammerhead and Zambezi **sharks** occur off the Mozambican coast, where shark nets are not in use. **Snakes** such as the deadly black mamba are not uncommon, but the chances of snakebite or shark attack are so small that they hardly warrant a mention. The bluebottle (or Portuguese man-of-war) belongs to a group of feeding polyps capable of inflicting a dangerous (but usually just very sore) sting. Floating around on a bubble, their long blue tentacles dangling in the water, bluebottles should be treated with caution even when washed up onto the beach.

CONVERSION CHART		
FROM	TO	MULTIPLY BY
Millimetres	Inches	0.0394
Metres	Yards	1.0936
Metres	Feet	3.281
Kilometres	Miles	0.6214
Kilometres square	Square miles	0.386
Hectares	Acres	2.471
Litres	Pints	1.760
Kilograms	Pounds	2.205
Tonnes	Tons	0.984
To convert Celsius to Fahrenheit: x 9 ÷ 5 + 32		

PUBLIC HOLIDAYS

1 January • New Year's Day
3 February • Heroes' Day
(Eduardo Mondlane died)
7 April • Women's Day
(Josina Machel died)
1 May • Worker's Day
25 June •
Independence Day
7 September • Victory Day
(Portuguese granted
independence)
10 November •
Maputo Day (effective in
Maputo only)
25 December •
Christmas Day

Easter Friday and **Monday**,
Boxing Day (26 December)
and **Samora Machel Day**
(19 October) are not really
official holidays, but many
businesses nevertheless close
on those particular days.
Muslim-run companies
can be expected to close
on the Islamic holy days.

Health Services

Many of the pharmacies in Mozambique dispense their medicines packed in brown envelopes and you have no way of knowing just what it is that you are buying, or its expiry date. Only in Maputo is adequate medical care available. If you are injured or become ill, you are strongly advised to make use of your medical insurance or, if seriously ill, have yourself evacuated to Johannesburg or your home country immediately. Although rural clinics are being refurbished, qualified doctors or other trained medical personnel may not be in attendance.

Personal Safety

Avoid the crowded areas in Maputo and Beira, and don't venture into badly lit places at night unless you are with locals. Poverty is rife and so is petty thieving, but backpackers and overlanders can relax at recognized camp sites which employ guards. Car hijackings and other armed robberies do occur, especially in Maputo, usually from the late afternoon onwards. Safe parking is scarce, but make an effort to seek it out, as vehicle parts, including windscreens and indicator lenses, are often stolen within minutes after you have left your vehicle.Groups of street children sometimes surround tourists and surreptitiously remove watches, wallets and other valuables from their unsuspecting victims. Without down-playing the horrific injuries that have been inflicted on Mozambicans by one of the most cowardly of modern weapons, the landmine, visitors who follow a few sensible precautions are far more likely to be stricken with malaria than come across **landmines**. A massive and thorough mine-clearing operation has already swept major roads, and is now concentrating on the minor ones and the more remote areas. Stick to well-used roads and trails, don't veer off and you will be safe.

Emergencies

Contact your embassy in the event of accident, theft or trouble with the law.

The police force and ambulance service generally are ill-equipped and trained. In Maputo call the police at tel: (1) 42-2001 and the fire brigade at tel: 198. For **private medical air rescue services** call: (Harare) tel: (2634) 73-4513 or (Johannesburg) tel: (2711) 403-7080/90.

Etiquette

Mozambicans value good manners and courtesy. Off the beach modest dress is expected. Before taking photographs of people, or entering private property, request permission. Customs officials and police are poorly paid and often expect a 'present' for prompt assistance. Rather than paying up, adopt a relaxed and unhurried attitude, which will confound the unscrupulous officials.

GOOD READING

• Newitt, Malyn (1994) *A History of Mozambique*. Wits University Press.
• Maclean, Gordon L (1996) *Roberts' Birds of Southern Africa*. John Voelcker Bird Book Fund.
•Sinclair, Ian; Hockey Phil & Tarboton, Warrick (1995) *Sasol Birds of Southern Africa*. Struik Publishers
• Moll, Eugene & Glen (1994) *Common Trees of Southern Africa*. Struik Publishers.
• Van der Elst, Rudy (1993) *Common Sea Fishes of Southern Africa*. Struik Publishers.
• Griffiths, Charles & Roberta (1993) *Seashore Life of Southern Africa*. Struik Publishers.

INDEX

Note: Numbers in **bold** indicate photographs